THE GOSPEL FOR LIFE

SERIES

THE GOSPEL &

Adoption

Also in the *Gospel for Life* series

THE
GOSPEL
FOR LIFE

— SERIES —

THE GOSPEL &

Adoption

SERIES EDITORS

RUSSELL MOORE *and*
ANDREW T. WALKER

PUBLISHING GROUP

NASHVILLE, TENNESSEE

978-1-4336-9032-7

Published by B&H Publishing Group
Nashville, Tennessee

Dewey Decimal Classification: 306.874
Subject Heading: BIBLE. N.T. GOSPELS \
ADOPTION \ ORPHANS

1 2 3 4 5 6 7 8 • 21 20 19 18 17

CONTENTS

Series Preface

Russell Moore

Why Should the *Gospel for Life* Series Matter to Churches?

IN ACTS CHAPTER 2, WE READ ABOUT THE DAY OF PENTECOST, the day when the resurrected Lord Jesus Christ sent the Holy Spirit from heaven onto His church. The Day of Pentecost was a spectacular day—there were manifestations of fire, languages being spoken by people who didn't know them, and thousands of unbelievers coming to faith in this recently resurrected Messiah. Reading this passage, we go from account to account of heavenly shock and awe, and yet the passage ends in an unexpectedly simple way: "And they devoted themselves to the apostles' teaching and the fellowship, to the breaking of bread and the prayers" (Acts 2:42 ESV).

I believe one thing the Holy Spirit wants us to understand from this is that these "ordinary" things are not less spectacular than what preceded them—in fact, they may be more so. The disciplines of discipleship, fellowship, community, and prayer are the signs that tell us the kingdom of Christ is here. That means that for Christians, the most crucial moments in our walk with Jesus Christ don't happen in the thrill of "spiritual highs." They happen in the common hum of everyday life in quiet, faithful obedience to Christ.

That's what the *Gospel for Life* series is about: taking the truths of Scripture—the story of our redemption and adoption by a risen Lord Jesus—and applying them to the questions and situations that we all face in the ordinary course of life.

Our hope is that churches will not merely find these books interesting, but also helpful. The *Gospel for Life* series is meant to assist pastors and church leaders to answer urgent questions that people are asking, questions that the church isn't always immediately ready to answer. Whether in a counseling session or alongside a sermon series, these books are intended to come alongside church leaders in discipling members to see their lives with a Kingdom mentality.

Believers don't live the Christian life in isolation but rather as part of a gospel community, the church. That's why we have structured the *Gospel for Life* series to be easily utilized in anything from a small group study context to a new member or new believer class. None of us can live worthy of the gospel by ourselves and, thankfully, none have to.

Why are we so preoccupied with the idea of living life by and through the gospel? The answer is actually quite simple: because the gospel changes everything. The gospel isn't a mere theological inquiry or a political idea, though it shapes both our theology and our politics. The gospel is the Good News that there is a Kingdom far above and beyond the borders of this world, where death is dead and sin and sorrow cease. The gospel is about how God brings this Kingdom to us by reconciling us to Himself through Christ.

That means two things. First, it means the gospel fulfills the hopes that our idols have promised and betrayed. The Scripture says that all God's promises are yes in Jesus (2 Cor. 1:20). As sinful human beings, we all tend to think what we really want is freedom from authority, inheritance without obedience like the prodigal son. But what Jesus offers is the authority we were designed to live under, an inheritance we by no means deserve to share, and the freedom that truly satisfies our souls.

Second, this means that the gospel isn't just the start of the Christian life but rather the vehicle that carries it along. The gospel is about the daily reality of living as an adopted child of a resurrected Father-King, whose Kingdom is here and is still coming. By looking at our jobs, our marriages, our families, our government, and the entire universe through a gospel lens, we live differently. We will work and marry and vote with a Kingdom mind-set, one that prioritizes the permanent things of

Christ above the fleeting pleasures of sin and the vaporous things of this world.

The *Gospel for Life* series is about helping Christians and churches navigate life in the Kingdom while we wait for the return of its King and its ultimate consummation. The stakes are high. To get the gospel wrong when it comes to marriage can lead to a generation's worth of confusion about what marriage even is. To get the gospel wrong on adoption can leave millions of "unwanted" children at the mercy of ruthless sex traffickers and callous abusers. There's no safe space in the universe where getting the gospel wrong will be merely an academic blunder. That's why these books exist—to help you and your church understand what the gospel is and what it means for life.

Theology doesn't just think; it walks, weeps, and bleeds. The *Gospel for Life* series is a resource intended to help Christians see their theology do just that. When you see all of life from the perspective of the Kingdom, everything changes. It's not just about miraculous moments or intense religious experiences. Our gospel is indeed miraculous, but as the disciples in Acts learned, it's also a gospel of the ordinary.

Introduction

Andrew T. Walker

AS YOU READ THIS BOOK, ONE THING WILL BECOME APPARENT: Adoption is one of the most important metaphors for the whole message of Christianity. It's a central feature of the story line of the Bible. Adoption helps explain the unconditional love of God as Father. Adoption helps explain how God can make rebels into sons by declaring us "sons" because of the work of God's Son, Jesus, whom the Bible calls our brother (Heb. 2:11). Adoption helps explain how people from across the globe and across history become the family of God. Adoption is an expression of the sheer willpower of God to create a family unto Himself that He's proud to call children (John 1:12).

How do we explain God's unconditional love? How do we explain the father motif throughout the Bible, and why is God's *being* a father so important to understanding who God is? How do unlovable, sinful people like you and me get grafted into God's family? How do we make sense of this community—the church—that transcends ethnic and political boundaries; this fact that God calls together a family consisting of people "from every nation, tribe, people, and language" (Rev. 7:9)?

Adoption is also an appropriate metaphor for the Christian's relationship and posture to the world. The book of James tells us that "pure and undefiled religion before our God and Father is this: to look after orphans and widows in their distress and to keep oneself unstained by the world" (James 1:27). The act of adoption is a vivid display of the type of love that God has for each of us. This is why, throughout the history of Christianity, Christians have always esteemed the dignity and worth of all persons. During the earliest centuries where Christianity was a small, unknown religion, its strangeness was displayed by its compassion amidst the all-too-common brutality of the Roman Empire. When in ancient times people would barbarically discard unwanted children, Christians took these children into their homes as their own. They didn't make distinctions between "adopted" children and "regular children." They were simply children.

This is why adoption represents the best of Christianity—it captures the center of Christian theology by revealing a God of unending love; and further, it puts to flesh the very ethics of Christianity. For these reasons we chose to include adoption in the *Gospel for Life* series.

But there's also a personal reason, for me, why adoption is in this series. In August 2008, I started working for Dr. Russell Moore. One of my very first assignments as an intern and research assistant was to help edit his book *Adopted for Life*. None of us who worked on that book knew of the success it would garner. The book has been credited with helping ignite an adoption movement across evangelical churches throughout America.

Regretfully, and to my embarrassment, at the time, I wasn't that excited about combing through a book looking for grammatical errors or typos. I also wasn't that excited about the topic itself. I thought to myself, *Adoption? Yeah, that's nice, but why dedicate a book to the topic?* I don't think I've ever been as wrong, ignorant, and misguided in my life as I was there.

Reading through that book, however, I was blown away at how consistently the adoption motif appeared throughout the entirety of Scripture. Despite my undergraduate degree in theology, I somehow glossed over the adoption metaphor in Scripture. I thought of it in academic terms, not visceral terms. To my thinking, "adoption" was a sanitized theological topic awaiting exegesis. It wasn't until reading that book that I began to realize that if it weren't for the adopting love of God, I'd have remained a hell-bound rebel.

So, it's with great excitement that this book in the *Gospel for Life* series focuses on adoption. We write for this book to be an introduction and entryway for you on how adoption is so central to Christianity. We know some who read this are contemplating adoption; others may have been given this book because your spouse is considering it, but you're entirely opposed to it.

The good news is that wherever you are in your journey, this book has something for you. As you'll learn in the book, not everyone is called to adopt children into their family, but every Christian has a part to play in fostering a culture of adoption that welcomes the unwanted.

Each book in the *Gospel for Life* series is structured the same: What are we for? What does the gospel say? How should the Christian live? How should the church engage? What does the culture say? We've structured the books this way so that every avenue of a Christian's life is addressed.

We hope you read with an open mind and an open heart about the centrality of adoption throughout the gospel and what God may be doing to call you, your family, or your church family into promoting a culture of adoption.

1

What Are We For?

David Prince

"THE FIRST TIME WE VISITED THE CHURCH, THE MOST STRIKING thing was the congregational diversity and that some of the families looked like a mini-United Nations. We thought, *I have never seen this before, and it is awesome.* We knew we had to come back to see what was producing this." Those are words of a family who had been visiting our church and decided to pursue church membership.

Our church has a strong emphasis on reflecting the gospel through an adoption culture where the entire church is involved in the rescue and care of orphans. The result has been the adoption of children from all over the world and many families in our church who are gloriously diverse.

Our adoption culture strengthens our church in many ways, but it most profoundly transforms how people think about theology, culture, and missions. An adoption culture provides a congregation with a beautiful and visible reflection of the gospel and ought to be understood as the natural consequence of a Christian worldview. Corporate worship in such a context provides a glorious theater displaying the power of the redeeming work of Christ. "Red, yellow, black, and white, they are precious in His sight," can be visibly witnessed even as it is being sung.

> Pure and undefiled religion before our God and
> Father is this: to look after orphans and widows in
> their distress and to keep oneself unstained by the
> world. (James 1:27)

As the father of eight children, when I speak at adoption conferences people always ask, "How many are adopted?" The answer is none. My family has not adopted, but we are passionate members of an adoption and orphan care movement and culture. J. I. Packer wrote correctly and succinctly about adoption saying, "the entire Christian life has to be understood in terms of [adoption]."[1]

Adoption in the Bible is not simply a matter of a few proof texts; it is woven into the fabric of the biblical witness. Paul clarifies that we are not simply to give mental assent to the gospel, but rather we are to conduct our lives "in step with the truth of the gospel" (Gal. 2:14 ESV). The practical outworking of physical adoption is inherent to Christianity. It is a nonnegotiable of walking in step with the gospel, and this is true for all Christians, not just those who become adoptive parents.

Adoption Is about Compassionate Dominion, Provision, and Protection

In the beginning, God uniquely instructed man to exercise *dominion*. The word simply means "to rule." God represents Himself at the beginning of the Bible as the King of the entire universe, and He declares that He created man in His own image to rule the cosmos under His authority. Man was to be His kingly representative on the earth and subdue it for His glory. The Bible paints a vivid picture of the kingly dominion of His image bearers,

> Then God said, "Let Us make man in Our image, according to Our likeness. They will rule the fish of the sea, the birds of the sky, the livestock, all the earth, and the creatures that crawl on the earth." So God created man in His own image; He created him in the image of God; He created them male and female. God blessed them, and God said to them, "Be fruitful, multiply, fill the earth, and subdue it [bring it into submission under My authority]. Rule

[have dominion over] the fish of the sea, the birds of
the sky, and every creature that crawls on the earth."
(Gen. 1:26–28)

This passage is a picture of man and woman's absolute
dominion over creation under the authority of God. They were
both given the responsibility to rule the world under the authority of God, but Genesis 2 clarifies that man was given the unique
responsibility to lead in the exercise of dominion. Genesis 2:18
explains that woman is to be man's "helper" in fulfilling the
dominion mandate. The dominion mandate includes man's
responsibility to be a provider through work (Gen. 2:8–15). Man
was to make the earth produce so he could provide for other
image bearers. It was—it is—a responsibility of protection and
leadership.

The Scripture teaches us that woman was created to be man's
helper in this dominion responsibility. The man was charged to
work the earth, and the woman was charged to be his helpmate.
This is a picture of the spheres of responsibility. Man was called
to lead in this effort, to be provider and protector. To those under
his care, man helps provide a sense of identity and an inheritance.
The command to exercise dominion compels man to say, "You
are who I am committed to protect. You are the one for whom
I will work and sacrifice. I will help you have a sense of identity
under God. I will give you an inheritance because you are those
whom God has given me."

The Fall and Fatherlessness

Immediately, however, we find Adam shirking his responsibility and leading his wife in rebellion. It is easy to miss; we often say, "What do you mean Adam is leading his wife in rebellion? The Bible says *she* is the one there with the serpent in the garden. He talks to her, and she eats the fruit from the tree of knowledge of good and evil, then she offers it to her husband. What do you mean he leads her into rebellion?" But, who was given the responsibility to lead and protect? Who was given the responsibility to lead in the dominion mandate? If there was to be a snake in the garden, it should have been on the ground with his head crushed, and there should have been a man with a bloody boot reassuring his wife, "I will take care of you." Yet, this isn't the case; the scene goes from dominion to rebellion and what we call the fall into sin.

The Fall

In the Fall, everything is twisted and contorted. Genesis 3 explains that Eve listens to the voice of the serpent while Adam, in his passivity, decides to follow rather than lead his wife. We find them listening to the voice of the Evil One over the voice of the King of the universe. The King says, "I will provide for you. You are My image bearers. Do you know what I'll provide for you? An inheritance of the whole universe; it is yours, rule it under My authority."

What happens? Genesis 3:6, "Then the woman saw that the tree was good for food and delightful to look at, and that it was desirable for obtaining wisdom. So she took some of its fruit and ate it; she also gave some to her husband, who was with her, and he ate it." They were essentially asserting, "I will establish my own identity. I will define what is good and live my life in light of what I define as good. The inheritance that I provide will be greater than what You provide. Thanks, God, but no thanks."

For the man's failed leadership in exercising dominion, God declares,

> And He said to Adam, "Because you listened to
> your wife's voice and ate from the tree about which I
> commanded you, 'Do not eat from it': The ground is
> cursed because of you. You will eat from it by means
> of painful labor all the days of your life. It will pro-
> duce thorns and thistles for you, and you will eat the
> plants of the field. You will eat bread by the sweat of
> your brow." (Gen. 3:17–19)

Understand what is happening. The whole cosmos was to be subdued under the authority of God; man's responsibility was to lead and create an entire civilization that sought its identity in God and received the inheritance God would provide. But, now even the ground is raging against the dominion of man; even the ground is thwarting man's ability to provide for himself and others. The whole world was thrown into chaos. Now, as a further consequence, there is the desire of a wife to rule over her husband and the desire of man to be oppressive rather than lead and care for his wife. All of these things are thrown into churning and rebellion. In this rebellion against God, there is the loss of both identity and inheritance.

Man is created in the image of God, but now the image is marred. The man and the woman are no longer recognized as God's own people. They have gone their own way and no longer have the blessing of the inheritance of an eternal kingdom. Having defiantly said, "I will produce my own kingdom," they experienced the loss of inheritance, but they also suffer the loss of identity. There is now sin, rebellion, murder, and deceit in the world. Identity no longer is found in God but in self-referential rebellion, which the Bible goes on to picture as slavery and bondage.

Fatherlessness

In other words, the fall into sin resulted in fatherlessness, because identity and inheritance is what a father is to provide. That is why the Bible keeps talking again and again about the horror of fatherlessness. There are constant biblical admonitions in this fallen world to care for the fatherless, to nurture the fatherless, and not to forsake the fatherless. It simply does not talk about the motherless in the same way. Why? Because it is easier to be motherless? No! It is awful, painful, and tragic; but in the biblical world, identity and inheritance came primarily from the father. To be motherless was to be pitied and to know the deepest pain, anguish, and agony, but it was not to be completely stripped of your ability to take care of yourself and to have future inheritance obliterated.

The father gave identity to the family, and as its leader he protected, provided, and said, "I will give my children an inheritance. It is yours because you are my children." To be fatherless is to have all the security for the future stripped away. The Bible says that man, in his rebellion, ended up no longer able to look to God and say, "Father." He had no identity; he had no inheritance—and this was not just true for Adam and Eve. It is true for every one of us if left to ourselves.

In other words—as a result of the Fall, the entire world became a spiritual orphanage, all of humanity in rebellion against God. We grope around in this world with the determination, "I will provide it for myself. I will go my own way. I will make a name for myself," and we find fallen man building towers to the heavens in order to build a name for himself, but it is an identity and an inheritance that would one day be swept away. But, God the Father would not leave man fatherless. God would graciously provide the answer to a world without an identity or inheritance.

We Are for Recovering a New Identity in Christ

Immediately after the fall into sin, there was a promise ultimately of adoption. Genesis 3:15 declares, "I will put hostility between you and the woman, and between your seed and her seed. He will strike your head, and you will strike his heel." It was foretold that there would be mighty blows, but only one blow would be fatal. This is the promise of the coming seed born of woman. The Bible keeps tracing the line that leads to that promised Son who would fulfill the gospel promise.

All the way through redemptive history, God is at work preserving that line. He kept raising up deliverers and saviors, all of whom pointed ahead to the one who was to come. Men like Abraham, Moses, and David were deliverers who have all kinds of flaws and failings, but they kept crushing the head of what represented the enemy of God. They remind us that there was another one coming who would crush the head of the serpent, fully and finally.

The Bible follows this line all the way to the Rescuer, the Deliverer, the Man, Christ Jesus. The Bible is very specific to point out that He is the Son of God who would come and reign and rule with a rod of iron, establishing dominion (Ps. 2:7–9). Hebrews 1:5 declares, about the one who was promised to come, "You are My Son." Why does it say that? Why is the Bible so clear that He is the promised Son? Because as the Son, He bore the identity of the Father. In fact, the Bible goes on to say, He was "the exact expression of His nature" (Heb. 1:3). He was the image bearer. You want to see the Father? Look at the Son. "The one who has seen Me has seen the Father" (John 14:9). He is the image bearer. The identity of the Father was clearly seen in the person of the Son, and it was the Son who would receive the inheritance of the Father.

How, in a fallen world of rebellion where identity and inheritance have been lost by sinners, can they ever be reclaimed? God sent His Son to establish perfect dominion. His Son always perfectly obeyed. His Son received all the blessings and favor of the Father. His Son, who had no sin, died for sinners so that they could be united to Him by faith. All who trust in the Son have their identity restored as His image bearers, adopted sons of God, who have an eternal inheritance provided for them.

In Ephesians 1, Paul declares that, in Christ, the believer as an adopted son has an eternal inheritance that cannot be taken away and is laid up for them in the heavens. He writes, "In love He predestined us to be adopted through Jesus Christ for Himself, according to His favor and will" (Eph. 1:4–5), and "We have also received an inheritance in Him, predestined according to the purpose of the One who works out everything in agreement with the decision of His will" (Eph. 1:11). You are brought into the family as adopted sons by sovereign grace through faith. Identity is restored and inheritance given. As much as God the

Father is committed to Jesus, He is committed to giving to those who are "in Christ" by faith. Theologian J. I. Packer has called adoption "the highest privilege the gospel offers . . . To be right with God the judge is a great thing, but to be loved and cared for by God the Father is a greater."[2]

In Hebrews 2:6–8, the writer quotes Psalm 8 to emphasize that God created man to rule and to reign. He asserts that everything was to be in subjection under man. But, there is a problem, "As it is, we do not yet see everything subjected to him" (Heb. 2:8). The good news is, "But we do see Jesus" (Heb. 2:9). Do you see the flow? Man is to have his identity in God and to have his inheritance provided by God. Yet, we do not see that. We see a spiritual orphanage of spiritually blank stares that are blind to the love of God. We see rebellion. We do not see man ruling the world under the authority of God.

In Jesus, we have identity and an eternal inheritance. Look at how it goes in Hebrews 2:6 (quoting Ps. 8:4): "But one has somewhere testified: 'What is man that You remember him, or the son of man that You care for him?'" The word *care* in Hebrews 2:6 is the same word in James 1:27, which is translated "visit" (ESV). What is man that You remember him, or the son of man that You visit him? What does it mean that God visits man?

Hebrews 2:7–8 continues, "'You made him lower than the angels for a short time; You crowned him with glory and honor and subjected everything under his feet.' For in subjecting everything to him, He left nothing that is not subject to him. As it is, we do not yet see everything subjected to him." The author describes how things are not under the authority and dominion of man to the glory of God. "But we do see Jesus—made lower than the angels for a short time" (Heb. 2:9). *But we see Jesus!* This is our gospel hope!

Hebrews 2:9 continues, "crowned with glory and honor because of His suffering in death" so that—and here is the purpose—"by God's grace He might taste death for everyone." Jesus came as the Savior, the Rescuer, the Deliverer. Notice Hebrews 2:10, "For in bringing many sons to glory, it was entirely appropriate that God—all things exist for Him and through Him—should make the source of their salvation perfect through sufferings."

What does it mean that God "visits" man? God visits man in his spiritual fatherlessness with no identity and no inheritance as a spiritual orphan. He comes and He dies for him; He rescues him; He delivers him, and through His love and self-sacrifice, we are sons of God. He is not ashamed to call us brothers (Heb. 2:11). There is a family relationship because of adoption. He makes us family by sovereign grace. This means that sinners whose identity was rebellion and whose inheritance was bondage are swept into the kingdom of God in Christ, and now by the witness of the indwelling Spirit, they call Jesus brother and God, "Abba, Father!"

This is the answer; Genesis 3:15 is fulfilled through what God has done and what He is doing through the Son granting identity and inheritance to sinners in Him (Heb. 2:17). That is why the Bible tells us that Christians cry out, "Abba, Father!" (Rom. 8:15; Gal. 4:6–7). On our own, we have no identity, no inheritance. In Christ, the Son of God, we become sons of God. Galatians 4:6 and Romans 8:15 both mention the "Abba" cry of desperation: "I need identity, I need inheritance!" Apart from identity and inheritance, we have no future and no hope. By grace, spiritual orphans become spiritual sons and experience all of the rights and privileges of sonship. That is the eternally good news—Jesus is willing by faith to embrace you as a brother and you can say with Him, "Abba, Father."

We Are for the Proclamation Gospel

How do we respond to this truth? We preach the gospel. We proclaim to the world this incredible gospel that you can be received into the family of God, that you can have identity in Christ and an eternal inheritance. Pastors and fathers are to lead congregations and homes in the task of evangelism, the gospel rescue plan. The Great Commission is the fulfillment of dominion mandate. Everyone is called to the task of missions, and men have a unique responsibility to lead. Followers of Christ must invade every corner of the global spiritual orphanage and preach the gospel hope that anyone can become a child of God by faith in Christ. This rescue mission will include dangerous and dark places, reaching out to those who are "not a people," but by God's grace can become "God's people" (1 Pet. 2:10).

Dominion is *already* restored when sinners "see" Jesus by faith (Heb. 2:9), and they live under His lordship in a fallen world, but it is *not yet* restored in the way it will be at the return of Jesus Christ as people are gathered from every tribe and tongue when Christ consummates His Kingdom. We must respond by preaching the gospel that God is at work in the fallen world saving sinners by faith from "the domain of darkness" and bringing them into "the kingdom of the Son He loves" (Col. 1:13), but many people want to stop right there. They say, "Amen, but stop. Keep it spiritual. That's what we should focus on, spiritual adoption. That's what matters most; that should be our focus."

Too many times we want to separate our lives into a divide of the spiritual and physical. There is an ancient heresy that never really goes away referred to as Gnosticism: the attempt to separate spirituality from the material and physical. Gnostic thinking is a constant threat that clouds and confuses Christians in every era. Spirituality, divorced from the physical and material, views creation, embodiment, people, and personal accountability as problems and obstacles to be overcome. The Bible refutes this idea of escaping the physical in favor of the spiritual at every turn. Creation, people, place, and history are not the problem;

they are the strategic setting for us to make much of Christ in our daily lives.

We Are for the Fatherless (Because We Were Fatherless)

What must the spiritually adopted—those who have been rescued, delivered, given an identity, and granted an inheritance—do? They must do nothing less than exercise dominion by working to reverse one of the most horrific realities of the Fall, *fatherlessness*. Churches, as outposts of the kingdom of Christ, must lead the way. Pastors, as the voice of Christ to their congregation, and fathers, as leaders in their families, must lead the way in adoption and orphan care. Rescued ex-orphans must be committed to leading the way in rescuing others, in seeing that others are granted an identity and an inheritance.

There are children right now, who do not know the phrase "Daddy" other than as an abstract concept. Identity? They do not have one. Inheritance? They do not have one. They don't have fathers. What they desperately need is a self-sacrificial Christian man to commit himself to their rescue and to look them in the eyes and say, "This is what a daddy looks like. You are mine. Your identity is bound up in our family and in who we are as a family in Christ. I will give you an inheritance. I am your father, and you are my child. I will not leave you as an orphan."

When someone rescued from the just judgment of God, spiritually adopted as a child of God, granted an identity and an inheritance by the grace of God, looks around the world and sees those who have been left fatherless by the Fall and says, "I will rescue you. I will be involved in providing you an identity, an inheritance," they are involved in exercising dominion and reversing an effect of the Fall to the glory of Christ's Kingdom. You see how that works? Physical adoption is a reflection of God's work of spiritual adoption in the lives of His people. It is a reflection of a people who are living out the supremacy of Christ in a fallen world (Col. 1:18). Taking dominion in the world by summing up all things in Christ (Eph. 1:10). Everybody who loves the Lord Jesus Christ is to be involved in rescuing orphans, and men are called to lead the way.

We Are for Visiting Orphans

If this is making you uncomfortable, you may be thinking, *He is making too much of physical adoption. He is just on a hobby-horse. I wish he would just focus on the gospel.* However, James 1:27 (esv) says, "Religion that is pure and undefiled before God, the Father, is this." We immediately expect something here, don't we? He is going to give us something spiritual; after all, spirituality is what is pure and undefiled. But, he throws us a curve. James says that religion that is pure and undefiled before the Father is this, "to visit orphans and widows in their affliction, and to keep oneself unstained from the world." Widows, like orphans, were particularly vulnerable and needy (Deut. 14:29; Ezek. 22:7; Acts 6:1–6).

The word *visit* is important. "Visit," in the Bible, is often used the way it is in this context, to visit for the purpose of caring for or rescuing (Gen. 2:21; 50:24; Exod. 3:16; 4:31; Josh. 8:10; Ruth 1:6; 1 Sam. 2:21; Zech. 10:3; Matt. 25:36, 43; Luke 1:68, 78; Acts 7:23; 15:14). When the Old Testament declares that God visited His people, it consistently means that He came to deliver them, to rescue them. Hebrews 2:6 (ESV) asks, "What is man, that you are mindful of him, or the son of man, that you visit him?" And what's the answer? Jesus. Hebrews 2:9 explains: Jesus visits His people to deliver them. He took on humanity and came to die for His people so that they might know the grace of God. He came to rescue His people. He came to bring "many sons to glory" (Heb. 2:10) and "That is why Jesus is not ashamed to call them brothers" (Heb. 2:11).

What does it mean to visit orphans? It means to care for them, rescue them, to bring them to the temporal glory of a gospel-loving family. It means to take those who have no identity and inheritance and to be involved in giving them an identity and inheritance. To visit the fatherless is to help deliver and rescue the fatherless by giving them a father. Men, you are called to lead the charge. Pure religion calls for courage and boldness. It is going to take courage to march into dark, difficult, and disease-ridden places, and say to a child, "You will be mine. All I have is yours." It is going to take courage to march in to some neighborhood in your own town and to a child who has all kinds of challenges and say, "You will be mine. All I have is yours."

Conclusion

James pulls the rug out from under those who desire to just keep adoption spiritual but not conduct their lives in line with the gospel. Many men pass off adoption as a woman's issue. Consequently, if you go to an adoption conference, you will often find the room is predominately filled with women. As one husband said to me, "Women care more about adoption because it is just their nurturing instinct." True enough, women are called and uniquely gifted to nurture. But men are called to protect, provide, and rescue. I wanted to look at him and say, "Nurturing instinct? Where is your rescuing instinct?" Those orphans need a courageous gospel warrior who will say, "I will gladly spend and be spent for your sake."

Listen to the way the Bible positions the issue of rescuing the fatherless. Psalm 68:1–5 describes God as a divine warrior, the One who came to rescue and deliver His people from fatherlessness. Notice the spiritual warfare imagery:

God arises. His enemies scatter, and those who hate
Him flee from His presence. As smoke is blown away,
so You blow them away. As wax melts before fire, so
the wicked are destroyed before God! But the righ-
teous are glad; they rejoice before God and celebrate
with joy. Sing to God! Sing praises to His name.
Exalt Him who rides on the clouds—His name is
Yahweh—and rejoice before Him. God in His holy
dwelling is a father of the fatherless and a champion
of widows.

This is the vision of pure religion He places before us to
reflect Him to the world as fathers to the fatherless. As we are
being conformed into the image of Christ, the Son of God, we
will increasingly reflect God's glory in the world. Churches that
constantly observe the power of the gospel reflect it in the pews
through adoption and listen to the sermon with a magnified
sense of expectation of the transformative power of the word
of Christ. Witnessing gospel passion and action that destroys
boundaries that legislation, political pressure, education, and
social action have not been able to budge is transformative and
cultivates a culture that expects God's Word to transcend the
cultural status quo.

A congregation built by gospel love that is reflected in the
rescue and care of orphans is a constant reminder that we are
a blood-bought church of King Jesus and not just an affinity

group. Not every Christian can or should become adoptive parents, but every Christian can and should be part of an adoption and orphan care culture committed to living out pure religion in gospel community.

Discussion Questions

1. Why is adoption and orphan care a gospel issue? What is the connection between caring for orphans and God's redemptive love toward His children?

2. Why do you think it's important to have the whole congregation embrace adoption and orphan care (adoption culture) and not just a few isolated individuals in the church (adoption ministry)?

3. What is dangerous about separating life into distinct spiritual and physical categories? What do we lose by doing this? What are some other ways this is done today?

4. The word *visit* is important in James 1:27. What does it mean? How might you visit orphans and widows as the outpouring of pure and undefiled religion?

5. Why is adoption and orphan care an issue for men and not just for women? What is unique about God's calling for men that would lead them to care for orphans?

CHAPTER

2

What Does the Gospel Say?

Russell Moore

MY WIFE AND I WALKED THROUGH THE DOORWAY OF A Russian orphanage. The squalor and stench of the place was such that we stifled the urge to vomit. We were led down a hallway with cracking floors and creaking stairs toward the room where two one-year-old boys were waiting in cribs to be received by us as our new children.[3]

A month and a half earlier we had been in that same orphanage every day for a week until we were told we had to go back home to the United States and wait until we received the call that all of the court work was done. We got that call and then spent three and a half more weeks in the former Soviet Union before they said that everything was finalized and we could receive our sons and take them home.

During those already-but-not-yet intervals, I had imagined what the scene might be like when we finally completed the adoption process. In my own mind, I guess I had thought it would be like a scene out of a movie: we would walk into the orphanage, our boys would receive us with joy and laughter, and we'd hug them and toss them in the air as music played in the background and we walked out and drove off into the sunset.

Needless to say, things didn't happen quite that way.

Instead, when we walked out of the orphanage with our two sons, they screamed. Up until this point, their entire life consisted of lying alone in their own excrement in a dark crib. Never before had they even seen sunlight. When we stepped outside for the first time, they had no idea what this brightness was, and they were terrified; they had never seen a shadow before, and tried to wipe them off their bodies as if they were bugs. When the wind blew into their faces, they winced. When we got into the car and the door shut, they screamed. And as we pulled out of the parking lot of that orphanage, both of them were shaking and red-faced—and they were lunging backward with arms outstretched desperately reaching back in the direction of the orphanage.

I leaned forward, not knowing what else to do, and whispered into their ears, hoping that the Russian driver wouldn't hear what I was saying (and knowing that the boys couldn't understand a word of English): "Relax, you have no idea. This place is a pit. You just have no idea what is waiting for you: family, Sunday school, Happy Meals, air conditioning!" But it didn't matter what I said. Those little hands were still reaching back for that orphanage. That place was horrifying. But it was all they had known, and it was home.

That was nearly ten years ago. The boys are now thoroughly Americanized. But I still remember those hands reaching backward. And I'm reminded how I've done the same and how the question of belonging is one the New Testament takes very seriously.

Adoption and the New Testament

The apostle Paul wrote a letter to some churches in Galatia that were fighting among themselves as to who really belonged in the church. They didn't know how they were going to live together and minister to the world outside their borders. Paul told them that they were not realizing the fact that they were all, each of them, ex-orphans. They did not understand that they had been adopted by the power of God. Paul told them that they had become God's children by God's adopting Spirit, but they were not able to see it because they didn't know who they were or where they were going. Because these churches lost sight of their identity and their future, they failed to understand the gospel and failed to grasp their mission as a church.

That is exactly what is at stake for us, as we understand what is going on with this idea of adoption. The imagery of adoption explains both the gospel and our mission, so we need to look carefully into what the Holy Spirit says about this adopting power of God and what it means for the church.

> For as many of you as have been baptized into Christ have put on Christ like a garment. There is no Jew or Greek, slave or free, male or female; for you are all one in Christ Jesus. And if you belong to Christ, then you are Abraham's seed, heirs according to the promise.
>
> Now I say that as long as the heir is a child, he differs in no way from a slave, though he is the owner of everything. Instead, he is under guardians and stewards until the time set by his father. In the same way we also, when we were children, were in slavery under the elemental forces of the world. When the time came to completion, God sent His Son, born of a woman, born under the law, to redeem those under the law, so that we might receive adoption as sons. And because you are sons, God has sent the Spirit of

His Son into our hearts, crying, "Abba, Father!" So
you are no longer a slave, but a son, and if a son, then
an heir through God.

But in the past, when you didn't know God,
you were enslaved to things that by nature are not
gods. But now, since you know God, or rather have
become known by God, how can you turn back again
to the weak and bankrupt elemental forces? Do you
want to be enslaved to them all over again? (Gal.
3:27–4:9)

In this passage Paul says that the adopting power of the
Spirit pictures the freedom of a new belonging. To be baptized
into Christ is to put on Christ. Paul is being very intentional in
telling these churches that they are all "sons." Remember, these
are people with thousands of years of Jewish heritage, who know
every page of the Scriptures and all of the promises that God
made to their ancestors. They know that they are the children
of Abraham, and they know that God is delivering the promises
that He has made to them through Jesus Christ.

The Gospel Grants a New Identity

But what these believers don't understand is the other group
of people in the congregation—the ones not like them. Those are
the pig-flesh-eating, uncircumcised Gentiles. They are the people

that in all of the Bible stories were the bad guys. But now those people are confessing that they believe Jesus is Lord, and some of the Jewish believers are responding by telling them they can be part of the church—they just need to be circumcised first.

Why were these Jewish believers doing that? Paul says they were doing it because they defined what it means to be the children of God according to the flesh, according to a person's genetic background as a child of Abraham, and according to those markings that you could make in your skin. But Paul refutes this. Becoming a child of God is not a matter of genetic inheritance, nor is it a consequence of some ritual your parents observed. Instead, Paul's ultimate argument is that if you are in Christ you are there by faith, and your identity is now in Christ. Christ's story is your story. Christ's heritage is your heritage, and Christ's people are your people.

That means that in Christ we are not identified as Jew and Greek, slave and free, blue collar and white collar, or any other way. Our identity in Christ is our true identity. It's a real family, albeit one not according to genetic material or bloodlines. But if God thought of you and me the same way many often think of adopted children—as somehow less real or less loved than the "normal" children—we would be in hell right now. The fact that God does not think of us that way is the very thing that makes our salvation possible.

Paul writes that the gospel that saves us is a gospel that took us out of our former identity that we used to have. We used to be someone else's children, and we behaved and acted just like our father, the Devil (1 John 3:10). But God adopted us and brought us into a new family in Christ. Paul goes even further, saying that if we are adopted into God's family, then we are also children of Abraham, because Jesus is Abraham's offspring. Our brothers and sisters are the people of the church because those are Jesus' brothers and sisters. He is bringing us into a new household and a real family. But if we're thinking in the flesh and according to the pattern of the world, this is hard to see.

The reason it is hard for us to see who we really are is that we often *want* to identify ourselves on the basis of the flesh, rather than on the basis of the Spirit. We are in Christ, and therefore sons of God, but that's not something that we can make true of ourselves on our own. Paul makes it clear that we aren't in this new family because of our flesh. This is the power of the Spirit at work in us to make us children of God. To be adopted into the family of God is to know God's free, saving grace.

The Gospel Grants a New Family

Right now, as you read this sentence, you are being called into a family by a Father who loves you, who wants to receive you, and who wants to say to you, in Christ, "You are My beloved son, and in you I am well pleased." Wherever you are right now, God has brought you to this moment—at your favorite coffee shop, in a third-world country, or in prison—for a purpose. You do not have to be an orphan in the universe. This reality should disarm the sinful pride in every one of us. None of us were born genetically into God's family. If we are part of God's family, it's only because God found us—helpless and abandoned on the side of the road—washed us off and took us home.

Why, then, during Sunday morning worship do we look around and grumble about what visitors are wearing or have inked on their skin? Paul says we were all slaves once, and we were all children of Satan. Why do we grumble among fellow believers about the most insignificant and petty of details when we have before us an everlasting inheritance? In Christ, we have a unity grounded in our shared identity in Christ, but too often we see ourselves and our preferences differently, and superior, even though we are all orphans adopted into God's family.

The Gospel Grants a New Cry

Paul writes that if we want to know who is in Christ, we don't look for people who have the sign of circumcision in their flesh. That means that we too shouldn't try to figure out who is part of God's family based on who has all of the same little religious markings, like who can find Hosea in a Bible without a thumb tab or who knows that the proper Christian answer to the question "How are you doing?" is "I'm blessed." The way we know we have been adopted into God's family is by the Holy Spirit's crying in us, "Abba!"

The Abba cry is about more than affection, however. It's a war cry. It's what the spirit of Jesus cries out in the Garden of Gethsemane, when He is about to be crucified and is in anguish, torturously asking His Father to take the cup of punishment away from Him. In our own lives, the Holy Spirit causes us to see and recognize a Father in the face of God, a Father who is with us as we live a life of repentance and grace, far beyond the singular moment of a "sinner's prayer."

Sometimes people will ask me, "Which of your children are adopted and which are natural born?" My response these days is to say that my wife and I don't keep track of that; we do not have any adopted children. Adopted is not an adjective in the Scripture—it's a past tense verb. God doesn't say to some Christians, "I love you, and you are Mine," and then turn to others and say, "I'm glad you're here, but you're just not as special."

I don't mind people knowing that we adopted our sons; in fact, I love the story of how we adopted them. But that doesn't define who they are any more than my fourth son, Jonah, is defined by the fact that he was born four weeks premature. I'm not ashamed of that. We don't hide it, but we don't identify him as "our premature son, Jonah." He is just our son. And the same is true of all of us as Christians. All of us are ex-orphans. But God brought us into a family, gave us a father, gave us brothers and sisters, and gave us a home. That's who we really are now.

The Gospel Grants a New Future

Not just that, but according to Paul we have also received a new future. We have an inheritance in Christ. The problem for an orphan isn't just that he doesn't know who he is or can't trace back his family tree. The problem is that there is no inheritance and therefore no future. The basic means of survival from one generation to the other is gone. An orphan without an inheritance is totally dependent on strangers to help him stay alive. That's what happened with the prodigal son; he took his father's inheritance and squandered it and had to work and eat among pigs, as a slave, because he lost his inheritance. That describes all of us. We were all slaves to the demonic powers and the appetites of our flesh.

Paul teaches us that God gave us the law so we could be hemmed in as children, until the time that we reach maturity and become heirs. But our impulse is to crave the slavery from which we were saved. Like the Jewish believers going back to the old circumcision and food laws, we want to return to the religiosity that is supposed to give us confidence, and try to live as though Christ never came. Or like the Gentiles, we want to go back to living as though we were in charge of our lives. We want still to act like orphans and slaves.

When my wife and I arrived home with our sons from the orphanage, the most difficult thing in our house for a very long time was mealtime. Now that's probably true for a lot of families with small children. But that is certainly true when you have one-year-olds who have never had solid food before in their entire lives. When food touched their mouths, they would start to gag. Because they weren't used to the regularity of meals, they would hide scraps in their chairs and sit with their fists up as they ate, terrified that someone would take the food away from them.

The moment Maria and I knew that these children were growing into our family was when their fists relaxed and they stopped hiding food. That meant they were starting to understand that we were their parents and would take care of them. The way these boys acted before they realized this is the same thing you and I do when we, who are in Christ and are going to receive an inheritance, instead act like orphans who have to fight for every scrap that we can get. This is exactly why many of us are so anxious and fearful about our future. We forget that now we're heirs, not orphans.

Adoption and Spiritual Warfare

Paul teaches us that the reason we are constantly drawn back to life as orphans is that we aren't just in a family; we're in a war. Our birth father, with his snake-like fangs, is still right outside the door, calling to us, "Don't you remember where you came from? Don't you remember what you're like? Don't you remember this is the way you have to be, the way that I am?" But the spirit of adoption says, "If anyone is in Christ, he is a new creation" (2 Cor. 5:17).

This new identity, and the spiritual warfare that surrounds it, isn't just about us. If we have received this adoption, then we must welcome and receive others even as Christ has received us. Paul's fellow apostle James writes in his epistle that true and undefiled religion in the sight of God is to visit orphans in their distress (James 1:27). So God is not just calling *some* of us to orphan care. There are many families who have adopted, or are foster parents, but according to Jesus this isn't a special "calling" just for those families. Scripture says all of us are going to be judged and held accountable before Christ for whether or not we recognized the face of Jesus in the least of these, his brothers and his sisters.

Right now, there are brothers and sisters of Jesus being ground to bits in bags marked "medical waste" only miles from wherever you are. There are children with cleft palates in India this moment who are being told no one could ever love them because of how they look. There are children in foster homes this moment who are hearing that no one will ever receive them into a home because they are beyond love. There are children waiting in orphanages and in group homes all around the world. And the mission of your church, and my church, and every single gospel church of the Lord Jesus is not merely to be glad when someone hears their cries. Everyone whose spirit cries "Abba, Father" can hear that same cry in others too. The spirit of adoption means we recognize the brothers and sisters of our Lord Jesus, and when we hear their cries, we do not simply turn away. We can't, because we were orphans too.

Conclusion

It very well could be that someone is reading this and God is actively calling them to adopt, but they're fighting the prodding and trying to out-argue the Holy Spirit. But it also could be the case that someone is reading and they're not being called to adopt, but they are being called to help someone do that. You might be called to babysit for couples while they go through the adoption process or the foster care process. Maybe you are called simply to pray with people in your congregation.

There are some Christians too who are genuinely children of God, but they are longing for slavery again. Maybe it's the thrill of hearing some new gossip. Maybe you cannot imagine what life would be like if you lived without pornography. Maybe the promise of being a child of God just isn't as exciting to you as the thought of being the most renowned or the most liked in your workplace. The gospel has a word for you: Repent, recognize that you are not an orphan anymore. Recognize that you are an ex-orphan who is adopted by the King of the cosmos. When all of those satanic powers want to destroy the "inconvenient," the "hopeless cases," and the "unlovable," it is the children of the King—not the sexual liberationists, not the secularists, not the world—who have to stand together and say, "Jesus loves the little children, all the children of the world."

Some day, probably when my two oldest boys are older, I plan to take them back to that orphanage where we first met them. I imagine they will be as sickened by that place as I was. But I want to take them there, and I want them to understand their story. And as we drive away I want to turn around and see a new sight, not babies reaching back in horror grasping for the orphanage, but young men looking forward into their future. Beyond that, I pray too that the church will see ex-orphans from every tribe, tongue, and nation headed toward a future inheritance, eyes forward, as their orphanages shrink in the rearview mirror.

Discussion Questions

· · · · · · · · · · · · · · · · ·

1. How does the imagery of adoption explain God's work in saving sinners? How does it picture the Gospel and Christian mission?

2. What does Paul teach about the identity and future of God's adopted children?

3. Do you ever feel drawn back to the tendencies of your old life? How does your status as a son or daughter in God's household effect how you view yourself?

4. None of us were born genetically into God's family. How does this eliminate pride and effect the way you see others? Does your own adoption influence the way you view those marginalized and unwanted by the world?

5. As ex-orphans, how should we think about these issues? What are some ways you and your church can get involved in adoption and orphan care? Are you open to what God is calling you to do?

How Should the Christian Live?

Randy Stinson

AS MANY CHURCHES ARE NOW TRYING TO BUILD AN ORPHAN care culture among its members, it is important to ask how a church can help when families actually begin adopting. Being burdened for orphans is one thing; bringing orphans into one's home and church is quite another.

Orphan Care versus Adoption

One of the first things a church can do is to emphasize the much broader scope of orphan care as opposed to the more narrow emphasis of adoption. The Bible admonishes us to care broadly for orphans and this could mean a whole host of options.

It may involve giving a financial gift to a local orphanage. It might mean helping a particular family bring a child home from another country. It might involve taking a mission trip to help an international orphanage. It could mean that the church contributes to an adoption fund that would assist the members of the church who are actually called to bring a child into their home. There are numerous other ways to care for orphans but the main point is for the church to create and highlight these options.

Churches that emphasize adoption to the exclusion or minimization of broader orphan care, many times inadvertently create a sense of guilt in those families who have decided that they are not in a position to adopt. In some cases, these families try and adopt anyway, believing this is the only meaningful way to participate. This often ends up creating unnecessary problems for the church and these families and, most importantly, the children that they brought into their homes. The church can't be silent on the issue of adoption nor should it perpetuate the idea that adoption itself is the only way for a member to be obedient to the James 1:27 admonition. Church members should be encouraged that no matter what stage of life, financial status, or family dynamic they find themselves in, that there are multiple, meaningful opportunities for them to participate in orphan care.

When this type of climate exists in the church, adoptive families and orphan care ministries flourish.

Equipping Those Considering Adoption

Churches can also help families as they prepare and pray about whether or not God is truly leading them to adopt. This, of course is a very significant decision and it is incumbent on churches to come alongside of their members to help prevent potential disappointment and disillusionment. Couples considering adoption must have the church come alongside them and help assess their motives. Some wrong motives include:

Guilt: Sometimes, when a family finds that a relative is giving up a child, it feels obligated to adopt in order to preserve its bloodline. Out of sheer guilt, the couple says, "We have to do it," because they can't imagine that the child would be in "someone else's" family. Relatives can be a wonderful fit, but certainly shouldn't be considered as the only alternative, especially if the family is adopting because of guilty obligation. It is often the case that a child thrives outside the immediate family. Adoptions based purely on family connections need to be considered carefully to help ensure that proper motives exist.

Other couples may feel pushed into adoption because their church is trying to create a culture of adoption and they feel guilty not doing "their part," so they adopt. Churches that are trying to create a strong culture of orphan care should make sure many options are available. Not only should there be many options, but the actual act of adopting should not be viewed as more important or more significant than the other ways of caring for orphans. It is also possible that a couple might desire to adopt from a general sense of guilt over its affluence. It may be better in some cases for the affluent family to help someone else adopt instead of doing it themselves. Guilt is certainly a biblically defined motivator, but it should not be the sole motivator in the case of adoption.

Romanticized adoption: Adoption is a feel-good act. During the adoption process, it is not uncommon for people to tell you what a great person you are and how they admire your willingness to sacrifice. People will tell you how special you are and how fortunate this new child is going to be to have you as their new family. You will hear of the many treasures in heaven you'll receive, and the list goes on. These are good words of encouragement from Christian brothers and sisters, but the church is responsible to help potential adoptive families keep their minds clear of an overly romanticized view. Just like a young couple that is dating can get caught up in the *idea* of marriage, a married couple can get caught up in the *idea* of adoption.

Marriage-builder adoption: One of the most common poor motives for adopting is the belief that the adoption will bring the marriage relationship closer. In a typical scenario, the husband and wife aren't doing very well. The husband is disengaged and the wife perceives that an adoption will naturally give them something to rally around so she initiates the process. For a time, it does seem to work. They have unified and common conversations as they get deeper into the process. His pseudo-reengagement seems real as he shows interest and even some involvement. They seem finally mutually excited about something. Then the child comes and the difficult task of parenting begins to take a toll creating tension and stress. For the husband, the "task" is over and he simply reverts back to his old disengaged ways. For the wife, she is now back to parenting alone, except now, she has another child to parent. Before you know it, the couple is right back where they began because of a weak foundation. Children are a wonderful blessing from the Lord, but they don't fix marriages. They should be the product of strong, healthy marriages.

Assimilating Adopted Children

Even if the right climate exists, a host of challenges present themselves to families who make the decision to adopt. One of the greatest challenges that adoptive families face is assimilating adopted children into the existing family. Churches would do well to make sure families have the instruction and encouragement and support needed to successfully assimilate a new child into the home.

Many parents think that this process begins the day the new child arrives, but that is way too late to begin assimilating. The process actually starts years in advance, especially if there are children already in the home. Over the years, we have learned that it takes a particular culture in the home to create the opportunity for the highest level of success. (I know that in some cases, it never actually works out no matter what, and that will be dealt with later in this chapter.)

Families must do the hard work of insisting on a culture of humility that treats others as more important than themselves. That begins with the marriage and extends to each member of the home. Adoption, at its heart, is a uniquely self-sacrificial act that requires what the apostle calls for in his exhortation to the Philippians, "Do nothing out of rivalry or conceit, but in humility consider others as more important than yourselves" (Phil. 2:3). Practicing this type of preference for others in everyday living begins to build a culture that assumes a willingness to lay down my own preferences for the good of others. If you don't want your current children to view the adoption as a rude intrusion into their particular patterns and lifestyle, then you must emphasize the axiom that my wife and I have repeated many times in our home: *inequity is the great equalizer.*

What this means is that everyone must be very cognizant of the fact that in the Christian life, aside from our status as children of God, there really is no such thing as *equity.* The apostle

Paul said that he learned to be content with much, and he learned to be content with little, which means that at various points in his life he had a lot, and at various points in his life he had very little.

A home that is set up for assimilating adopted children has learned to minimize things like sibling rivalry. Sibling rivalry and jealousy are exacerbated by a parenting strategy that tries to make everything equal in the home. If one kid gets a pair of shoes, the other kid gets a pair of shoes. If one kid gets a piece of candy, the other kid gets a piece of candy. To many parents this seems, intuitively, to eliminate rivalry and jealousy since there is no opportunity for inequity. In actuality, it creates just the opposite. Parents who try to make everything equal establish an entitlement mentality. When one kid receives a gift of candy, the other kids not only begin to expect a piece of candy, but begin to believe they are entitled to it. Unfortunately, as parents utilize this failed strategy, they end up creating the very environment they hoped to avoid.

Instead, parents should teach a theologically grounded understanding of the world, which rejects an entitlement mentality. Children must learn not to view the world through a lens of self-referential fairness but rather through a lens of grace. As Paul writes, "What do you have that you didn't receive? If, in fact, you did receive it, why do you boast as if you hadn't received it?" (1 Cor. 4:7). This grace lens is how God instructs us to view the world as we live with one another. God graciously doles out His good gifts in perfect wisdom as He pleases. A home that is characterized by this others-oriented grace is more apt to be able to deal with all of the inefficiencies of bringing a new child into the home.

Another key element in assimilation is helping the adopted child understand their particular story. While we never want to ignore or minimize a newly adopted child's background, we also want to make sure that we don't make it the focus of and prescription for how we parent.

One of the mistakes we have seen parents make over the years is to dwell too much on the adoption side of the equation. This can be seen when parents introduce their children as the "adopted" ones or when parents insist that their "adopted" kids be around other "adopted" kids. It also can affect a parent's willingness to give or withhold discipline. Often, the latter is more the case. The faster your child learns that they are welcomed and loved and just as much a sinner in need of discipline and grace just like all the other kids in the home, the faster they will assimilate into the family. When we constantly focus on the "adoption," we are reinforcing the fact that he/she is different from the other kids. The lines should be blurred, not consistently underscored. Your child's adoption is a one-time event and, while it is certainly a significant event in their life and story, it should not be the filter through which all things flow.

When assimilation is put off until the arrival of the child, or pre-adoption counseling is absent, challenges can arise. Parents may begin to align themselves with their biological kids, taking up offenses for them and making assumptions based on emotions rather than facts. This creates an "us against them" environment, which sets the stage for potentially significant problems.

Managing Expectations

Churches should also play a strong role in helping adoptive families manage expectations. Sometimes parents are disillusioned because they have false expectations about how the adoption should go after they get the child home. Discouragement ensues and often can cause doubt in the mind of the couple as to whether or not they should have adopted in the first place. This can be a very weighty burden that can put the couple in a situation with no one to talk to. Church leaders should understand some of the potential wrong expectations of newly adoptive families so that they might identify some problems earlier rather than later. Some wrong expectations include:

Hallmark moment(s): Sometimes a family will adopt a child and it doesn't experience the Hallmark moment. They are often preoccupied with the good feelings often associated with adoption and when those feelings subside, or never appear in the first place, discouragement sets in. They haven't really counted the cost to realize that many times adopted kids don't sleep through the night, don't obey, don't necessarily feel gratitude toward you, and may have experienced difficulties in their former situation that are unknown to the adoptive family. Parents become disillusioned when they don't immediately see evidence that this is all going to end "happily ever after." Churches would serve adoptive families greatly if they could anticipate this challenge and learn to recognize it early.

A quick transition: When a husband and wife get married, it takes some time to make the adjustment to living under the same roof. Adoption is similar. Couples shouldn't expect a quick transition. It may take a while. It may take even years. This can become a source of frustration for parents. We counsel couples to adjust their lives so that they can be locked down for a year. What we mean is that we don't do much travelling. We don't do much socializing in other people's homes. We don't leave our newly adopted kids in the care of others all that much. The older the child, the longer it may take before they are comfortable and secure. Don't expect some kind of immediate, smooth transition.

Immediate gratitude: Just because you've rescued a child, don't expect him or her to know it or appreciate it immediately. Having a new pair of Nikes and their own bedroom is not going to immediately overcome the challenges of a new place absent from everything they have known (even if it was something you would consider "a bad situation"). Sometimes families falsely assume that because they "rescued" their adopted children from what they would consider to be a difficult future, they will immediately show verbal and physical gratitude, but the adoptive children don't always see it that way. This is especially true the older the child is. Their past is the only experience they've ever known and they will often yearn for the place from which they came even if it was a difficult place. They are often afraid to share these feelings for fear that they will hurt you or that their security will be in jeopardy. Discouragement will occur when parents are personally offended at this very natural reaction.

What If It All Goes Wrong?

In a fallen world, there are innumerable patterns of sin that can occur in the life of any human being. Sometimes children, both biological and adopted, yield to sin in ways that are heart breaking and sometimes unimaginable. Adopted children who end up being behaviorally intolerable can be more complicated because sometimes their past is complex or even unknown.

Parents can be working off of very little or nonexistent medical and family history, which further complicates the matter. Parents may find themselves in a situation where they may need to remove the child from the home, hopefully temporarily but maybe even permanently. This should not terminate the adoption. Parents should walk through this scenario just as they would with a biological child. Church leadership must think through this scenario thoroughly in advance so that they can give wise counsel to families who are in this crisis. Along the way, I've learned a few things about crisis adoptions of which churches need to be aware.

First, churches should believe adoptive parents when they are told about what's going on in the home, unless they give the leaders a reason to think they are untrustworthy and deceptive. Often problem children can be manipulative. They might be incredibly difficult at home but very sweet in public. In many situations, churches may only see the child in certain public situations and wonder if the parents are exaggerating their story or may have too high of expectations. This has a way of making families feel isolated because they surmise no one acknowledges the problems they face or at the very least no one is taking them seriously. Churches should guard against this type of response in a crisis adoption.

Second, churches must find various ways to help families going through crisis adoptions. Many larger churches have ministries that help provide resources for adoption and orphan care. But in most churches, only one or two families adopt at a given time. In these cases, it's incumbent on a church to come alongside the family and help network and gather resources. Churches should make themselves aware of other ministries that are specifically geared toward helping adoptive families work through post-adoption challenges. They should be aware of other churches that may have a larger adoption culture that may be able to connect the families in one church to families in other churches. Some of the challenges adoptive parents will face are simply the same challenges all parents face. Other times, the problems are clearly adoption-related and it is necessary to have someone with specific experience to help the family in crisis. Churches would do well if they partnered with a network of churches and other credible ministries, with adoption expertise, to help address those challenges.

Third, sometimes parents and the adopted child do not attach and bond right away. This may take years. It may never happen to the degree that the family expected or had hoped for. It may be that the child just can't or won't do it. It also might be that because the parents were disillusioned about some aspect of the process, they have thwarted the attachment process. The exact reasons and explanations can be very complex but in the end, churches need to come alongside the adoptive parents and help guide them through this problem like they would any other host of challenges. Paul told the Thessalonians to "warn those who are irresponsible, comfort the discouraged, help the weak, be patient with everyone" (1 Thess. 5:14). Churches will have to exercise great wisdom in these cases. Some situations will require that parents just exercise a level of patience that heretofore has not been required of them. Others may require a different parenting strategy. Still others may require a rebuke or act of discipline. May God give churches the wisdom and discernment needed to navigate these sometimes very difficult waters.

Pre-Adoption Counseling

Many years ago, churches realized that there was a high divorce rate among Christians and as a result put into place a series of conversations to be had with engaged couples. In what is usually called premarital counseling, couples work through a series of topics to help prepare them for married life. The primary goal is to help create proper expectations based on the collective wisdom of what the typical newlywed couple deals with. Most likely the counseling will address how to deal with disagreements regarding finances, conflict with in-laws, arguments, and other such issues.

Churches need to realize that adoption brings about its own unique set of problems and challenges and institute some sort of pre-adoption counseling that would prepare potential adoptive parents, much like premarital counseling prepares engaged couples. Pre-adoption counseling should be about asking good questions. Probably the most important question to ask potential adoptive parents is, "Why are you adopting?" As mentioned earlier in this chapter, this is one of the most fundamental questions that can help to assess motive. It can also help assess unity between husband and wife. Many times a wife will be excited about adoption and the husband will not share the same level of excitement, but they will press on in spite of the lack of mutual desire. There needs to be great unity if a couple is going to proceed. Sometimes it just takes a little longer for a husband to embrace the idea. In other cases, he may never agree. Either way, churches must help give the best wisdom.

Couples need to ask if they have enough financial margin in their life. Adoptions can be very expensive, and counting the cost of such a venture is a biblical admonition (Luke 14:28). Couples should decide if they have the emotional margin to adopt. This is similar to the financial question. Some families have the adequate finances but lack the emotional resources. Adding an adopted child many times brings unique challenges that require even more energy and patience than a biological child. Money is not the only limited resource. Some people have more emotional capacity than others, and this is another area where churches should help their members by helping them assess their ability to add more children. If a family already has a chaotic and poorly deployed parenting strategy and consequently are stretched too thin, it may not be best for them to adopt. They also need to be asked what will happen if/when the child they bring home has unknown health, behavior, or cognitive issues. Do they have support or are they receiving pushback from family and friends? These are questions that the church can come alongside and help families considering adoption think through. Church leaders put steps into place before a couple gets married in their congregations. We ought to put something similar into place for adoptive parents.

Post-Adoption Care

Post-adoption care is about intentionality. In many churches, when a couple gets married, there's a newlywed class for them. We ought to offer something similar to families going through adoption. At the very least, church leadership should be checking back in on a couple after the adoption. Sometimes parents are going through a crisis and may feel embarrassed by it. That's why church leadership must be proactive and come alongside these families. I know a family who has adopted several children and had relatively smooth transitions with each of them. Later, they adopted another child and this child has challenged them in a way they've never dealt with before. The couple became embarrassed and struggled because they thought they should be able to handle all the adoptive issues that had arisen. As fellow church members, we need to press in on them, not in an intrusive way, but in a loving, caring way to say, "We know there could be some challenges, tell us what they are, we'll help you walk through them."

Conclusion

Adoption and its centrality to the gospel has made it a growing movement in the church. Just like other movements, the church not only needs to pursue it, but make sure it is examining the movement to ensure it is rightly positioned to offer correctives and solutions for problems that will naturally occur. The church cannot naively assume that the most difficult part of an adoption is the process that leads up to it. It also cannot assume that every couple that has a desire to adopt should be able to do it. Orphan care begins when the church takes the time to think of the child's best before they even arrive. Sometimes the child's best means a church has to do the hard task of saying, "We don't believe you're ready." But for those families that the church identifies as ready, they must count the cost, do the hard work in advance, and be willing to humble themselves by seeking help. May God be pleased to strengthen families who have embarked on the incredible adventure of adoption, and may He use the church and its leaders to do so.

Discussion Questions

1. How does a church cultivate an environment that prioritizes orphan care? Why is this an issue everyone in the church can and should be involved with? How might the

distinction between general orphan care and the specific act of adoption help people see this?

2. Why should couples considering adoption look carefully at their motives? How can hidden motives actually undermine families and ultimately cause more harm than good?

3. What does it mean to view everyone through a "lens of grace" and how can this help in the process of assimilation? How does a theologically grounded understanding of the world reject entitlement?

4. Why is pre-adoption counseling important? What are some of the most common (and faulty) expectations about adoption? How can churches help couples manage these expectations?

5. Post-adoption care is often forgotten in discussions about adoption. How does a holistic approach to orphan care prevent this potential oversight and what can the church do for families experiencing a "crisis adoption"?

4

How Should the Church Engage?

Jedd Medefind

FROM THE FIRST DAYS OF THE EARLY CHURCH, CHRISTIANS were known for caring for the children no one else wanted. The church has engaged from the very beginning of the Christian movement.

How the Church Has Engaged

Ancient Romans had a way to get rid of undesired babies. They called it "exposing." Whether malformed, the wrong gender, or simply inconvenient, the child was taken outside the city. Sometimes it was thrown into water to drown. Other times, it was left for the sun, storms, or wild animals to do their work.

But the early Christians could not accept this. They believed God formed every child and each was precious. They earned a reputation for going outside cities to find these children, take them in, and in some cases even raise them as their own.

This commitment helped define the early church. Pastoral candidates were required to be known as "lovers of orphans."[4] Some individuals, like the former prostitute Afra of Augsburg, formed networks of Christians to receive and adopt unwanted children.

The contrast with the surrounding culture was stark. Greek and Roman gods had little concern for any but the swift and the beautiful, the athletes, queens, and generals. Ordinary people were expendable; the weak were despised. Little wonder the Roman philosopher Seneca stated matter-of-factly, "We drown children who at birth are weakly and abnormal."[5]

But the God claimed by these early Christians viewed human life differently. He cared for all, especially the weak. He not only called His people to look after orphans; God described *Himself* as a "defender of the fatherless."

Little wonder Christians sought to do the same. And whenever they did, they put the character of their God on vivid display. They made His grace touchable. Their God was utterly different from any pagan god—and so were His people. The premium they placed on the children others tossed away shone bright. It contrasted like beacon fires against life-demeaning values of cultures around them.

The sixth-century Code of Justinian shows how this vision began to pervade Roman culture as Christianity's influence rose. The Code—often said to be the foundational document of Western legal thought—banned exposing and other forms of infanticide. It required that orphaned children not be taken in merely as household help, but rather "treated with Christian care and compassion."

Finally, Justinian's Code urged that orphans in need of families be adopted "even as we ourselves have been adopted into the kingdom of grace."[6]

How the Church Is Engaging Now

Committed Christians in every century have shown special concern for children on the margins. But it is hard not to notice a vibrant rekindling today. Some of these efforts center on adoption; others on foster care. Still, others on supporting orphan care overseas. Often, it is all of the above.

The *New York Times* observed that Christians "have increasingly taken up orphan care as a tenet of their faith." *Time* magazine headlined, "A Church Movement to Give Every Child a Home." *Christianity Today* labeled it the "burgeoning orphan care movement."

In Arkansas, a wide network of churches named "The CALL" now provides more than half of the state's foster parents. Colorado churches have helped cut the number of children waiting to be adopted by more than 50 percent. Similar church movements can be seen from Oregon to Florida to Washington, DC. Meanwhile, each of the past four years, giving to orphan care by Christians has grown at a rate *three times* that of American charitable giving generally.[7]

Increasingly, churches worldwide are also stepping up for orphaned children. Ukrainian Christians have adopted thousands of children from local orphanages. Rwandan churches have helped dramatically cut the number of children growing up in orphanages. From the Philippines to Zimbabwe to Guatemala, visionary pastors are challenging cultural biases against both orphans and adoption.

In each of these places and many others today, Christians are living out a vision that blazes in bright contrast to common assumptions and priorities of the cultures around them, just like the church in Roman times.

Fostering a Movement

Possum Trot isn't even a dot on most maps of west Texas. Like Nazareth, it's a place you might not expect much of. No paved roads or streetlights. The largely African American church, Bennett Chapel, tops out around two hundred on an average Sunday. But it has made an outsized difference for kids who previously bounced from home to home in the foster system.

In 1996, something stirred the heart of Bennett Chapel's pastor, Bishop W. C. Martin, and his wife Donna. Donna sensed God's whisper, "Think about all those children out there who do not have the love you had from your mother."

The Martins already had two children. At first, W. C. merely tolerated his wife's efforts to bring in a girl and boy from the foster system, Mercedes and Tyler. Then he met them. On his first visit to the house, two-year-old Tyler ran to W. C. with a shout of "Hey, Daddy!" and wrapped him in a hug. From that moment W. C. and Donna were in it together, venturing the joys and challenges of loving children from hard places.

But that was just the beginning. Other families noted the Martins' choices. W. C. explains, "The idea of reaching out to orphans was no longer a far-off notion. These were orphaned kids sitting right beside them in the pews." It began spilling out in W. C.'s sermons, too. "God commands us to take care of the orphans. The power lies in the hands of the church," he declared.

Ultimately, the Martins adopted Mercedes and Tyler, then their siblings, Terri and Joshua. Family after family followed suit. Today, seventy-six children have been adopted at Bennett Chapel.

This shows what even small churches can do. And consider this: If each church in America adopted just *one* child from foster care, there'd be more families waiting for children than children waiting for families.[8]

W. C. and Donna don't sugarcoat it. There's been heartbreak, too, and countless unsung days of weary plod. But they will tell you the sacrifices have been more than worth it—far more. The joy of seeing crumpled children blossom; the rich texture of family life together; and countless lessons in grace revealed by children who have come home with deep wounds.

All this has transformed not only hurting children—it has drawn many families and the church as a whole nearer to Christ as well. As W. C. puts it, "They are teaching us a God kind of love."[9]

Where Do We Start?

When we've caught this vision, we want others to see it too. But often our enthusiasm resorts to the same motivators used by any good "cause." After all, what do most appeals for giving or involvement boil down to: duty, guilt, and idealism. "We really *ought* to do something. Don't you *feel badly* for how little they have? Won't it be *great* when we solve this?" These are powerful motivators, and each can be warranted at times.

But charging out to love orphans nourished only by duty, guilt, or idealism is like trying to cross the Sahara Desert with one canteen of water. The inevitable complexity and disappointments will leave us withered and dry. The world's hurt will always outlast mere enthusiasm to solve it.

So in seeking to motivate others and cast a vision in the church, we should not start with statistics of vast need or photos of demoralized faces. Yes, there is a time to puncture apathy by telling frankly of the world's hurt. But that is not where we must begin. While the need is real, and the Bible is unequivocal in its command to care for those in distress, the ultimate motive runs even deeper.

For the Christian, the wellspring of all love and service is *the Story*, the wonderful, true story of the God who goes outside the city walls to find us when we are destitute and alone. At immeasurable cost, He pursues and embraces us. He invites us to live as His children, possessing a full share in His identity and inheritance. Only then does God invite us to go and love in like manner.

Far more than a *requirement*, caring for orphans is first a *response* to God's love. It is not just a *mandate*, but a *mirror* of God's character. Long before Isaiah reminded God's people to "defend the rights of the fatherless" (1:17), the Torah describes the Almighty with those same words, "He defends the cause of the fatherless . . ." (Deut. 10:18 NIV). He is for the orphan. And He is for us.

Rooted here, in God's redemptive story, adoption and orphan care are never merely a "cause." Rather, they spring from discipleship: a lifelong journey of growing more like Jesus. Such a culture—or, we might say, *counter*culture—rises when people come to know, rejoice in, and reflect the heart of their Father.

Growing as disciples causes us to care for orphans. And caring for orphans causes us to grow as disciples.

Understanding the Need

To serve others wisely and well, we must first understand the contours of their need.

An estimated 17.6 million children worldwide have lost both parents.[10] Nearly ten times that number meet the official definition of "orphan," having lost at least one parent. Millions of others—sometimes described as "social orphans"—live without parental care as a result of abandonment, abuse, severe poverty, or other factors. In the US, currently 415,000 children live in the foster system—removed from their biological family as a result of abuse or severe neglect.

The biblical understanding of the "orphan" or "fatherless" encompasses all of these children.[11] It is the girl or boy who has lost the full protection, provision, and care that God intended parents to provide.

Each has a unique story. Their needs and ideal solutions vary greatly. But we must know this: *children growing up without a family are the most vulnerable beings on our planet.*

These boys and girls face virtually every evil known to man at dramatically increased rates—from disease to exploitative labor to loneliness. They lag behind other children in everything from height and weight to cognitive development.

This is true even in nations that pour billions of dollars into welfare systems like the US. The futures awaiting children who "age out" of US foster care without being adopted are tragic. By their mid-twenties, less than half are employed. More than 60 percent of males have been incarcerated as adults, versus 9 percent of men overall.[12] With women, 68 percent are on food stamps, compared to 7 percent overall.[13] They experience PTSD at rates double those of returning combat veterans.

The vulnerability of children without parents is especially vivid when it comes to human trafficking. A study in Moldova found that girls who grow up in orphanages are ten times more likely to be trafficked than others.[14] An assessment in Zambia found that three quarters of all child prostitutes were orphans.

Their average age was fifteen. These children had sex with three to four clients on an average day.[15]

This does not happen only in far-off places. In a 2013 raid of US trafficking operations by the FBI, 60 percent of the child victims rescued were foster youth.[16] Is it any wonder that God calls His people to step in here, to stand between these children and all the evil that desires to prey upon them?

The Priority: Family

When we see such vulnerability and hurt, our hearts break. We yearn to act. And as we grasp the vastness of the need, it's natural to want to respond on scale to match it.

That's why in the past, when big-hearted people heard about orphans, their first thought was to build an orphanage that could house hundreds of children. That's sometimes the case today, too. It's natural to try to meet a mass need with a mass response.

But more and more, social science is confirming what Scripture has always taught: *God designed family as the best place for a child to grow.*

Family is God's idea. Family is His ideal. Right after describing God as a "Father of the fatherless and a champion of widows," Psalm 68:6 expresses, "God provides homes for those who are deserted."

Even before birth, a child's brain develops at an astounding rate, with billions of neural pathways formed. The pathways that are well used expand into superhighways for thought, emotion, and language. But those that aren't used atrophy and disappear. So the things any caring parent provides—response to a baby's cry, affectionate touch, play, eye contact—literally hardwire a child for relationship and successful living. Their absence does just the opposite.

This helps explains the significant delays in children's mental development measured in orphanages across many different regions of the world.[17] Other studies show that in orphanages that provide little personal affection and care, children are significantly smaller than average—even when all their physical needs are met![18]

The importance of a nurturing family does not disappear as children grow. I think of a vibrant young woman named Chey who spent time in Tennessee foster care. At fifteen, she landed a job and bought an old car to get her to and from work. But one day while driving on the interstate, the car began to lurch as smoke poured from the engine. She steered onto the shoulder and sprang from the car to safety. But the engine was destroyed. As Chey explained to me later, "I knew you needed to put gas in the engine, but no one ever told me about the oil."

Even in adulthood, the significance of family does not disappear. Friends who grew up in orphanages or foster care have often shared with me the loneliness they feel without a family to come home to, especially at holidays. As a friend who aged out of foster care shared with me in his mid-thirties, tears in his eyes, "You never outgrow the need for a family."

This truth should never be lost to Christians. We see the beauty of family affirmed throughout Scripture. We experience it in God's embrace of us as adopted members of His family. So Christians of all people should not turn reflexively to institutions. We should be known as champions of family first.

Of course, like every area of deep human need, the ideal isn't always in reach. In many parts of the world today, well-run children's homes provide a vital alternative to life in abusive situations, on the streets or worse. Thoughtful advocacy for orphans can *both* honor the devoted care provided by many quality residential facilities *and* champion family as God's best for children.

What does that look like? Here are the basics, whether in the US or globally:

> *First, preserving families.* Helping at-risk families to stay together. This can range from training in parenting skills to micro-business opportunities to help parents provide for their children.
>
> *Second, reuniting families.* Rejoining families, as long as this won't put children in danger. This often requires

helping parents overcome root issues that caused the split and oversight to make sure children are safe.

Third, growing families. Placing children into loving new families when reunification with biological parents or placement with relatives aren't possible.

Only when these three options are out of reach should we turn to other solutions. And even then, family must remain our North Star. Any proposed solution should be as close as is feasible to the ideal of safe, permanent, nurturing family.

The Church at the Center

This need for family creates a major dilemma. It's a mass-scale problem that defies mass-scale solutions.

Governments and other large institutions can marshal huge volumes of material things like food, housing, and medicine. And effective child protection systems can reduce neglect and abuse. But while these all can be vital to enabling vulnerable children to survive, children require much more to thrive. Children need most of all love, nurture, and belonging. These cannot be created by government fiat or manufactured on assembly lines.

Government agencies are full of dedicated, overloaded workers doing their best to protect children from harm. Christians should publicly honor and support these women and men

(Google "National H.E.L.P. Week" for ideas as to how). But professionals alone can't provide all that children need. As a thirty-year veteran of state child welfare, Dr. Sharen Ford, once lamented to me, "Government makes a terrible parent."

So here is a simple truth: the church cannot outsource James 1:27. Government shouldn't *have* to be a parent. And when the church is doing its job, government doesn't *need* to be a parent.

The data bears this out. Practicing Christians adopt at rates more than double the general population.[19] They also foster at rates roughly 50 percent higher than the general population.[20] They're also willing to welcome older children and those with special needs at higher proportions as well.[21]

Churches still have immense room for growth in this. But when government looks to find caring families open to fostering or adopting, it can't do better than starting with a church.

Not Just One Family

For churches to be a source of foster or adoptive families is no small thing for child welfare. But a church has resources of even greater significance.

Consider: nearly half of foster parents quit within a year of their first placement.[22] Why? Because it's hard. Like the deep human needs it seeks to address, the foster system itself is tangled and frustrating. The approval process is tedious. Regulations often feel arbitrary. Doctor visits, counseling sessions, court dates, and other appointments upend family schedules. And, perhaps most of all, sharing one's life and private space with a child in need of healing can be exhausting.

The same can be said of adoption. Many adoptive parents struggle, especially when unprepared for all that is required to nurture a child who has experienced trauma or has special needs.

Here is a reality we must never forget: *every child's journey as an orphan or in foster care began with a tragedy.* And usually it gets worse from there. Most of these children have experienced the world at its most broken. The people who should have loved them most have died . . . or abandoned them . . . or inflicted harm. Very likely, others have done the same.

Little wonder, when we welcome hurting children into our lives—alongside the unparalleled gifts they bring—we will taste some of their hurt as well.

Adoption and foster care are not solve-a-problem-from-far-off propositions. They come near, open themselves, become vulnerable to the very pain they seek to salve. They offer an unparalleled opportunity to "know Christ . . . the power of his resurrection and participation in his sufferings" (Phil. 3:10 NIV).

Embracing the orphan mirrors the gospel story—not only in its beauty, but also in its costliness.

This is a journey not to be walked alone. So a healthy culture of adoption and orphan care does not emphasize, "One child embraced by a loving family." Rather, the vision must always be, "One child embraced by a family embraced by an entire church."

And here's the great news: God *designed* the church for this! When the church is not doing this kind of thing, it is not living out its purpose. It becomes a sad, flaccid creature compared to the robust community God intended. But when a local church starts to exercise the muscles required to support foster and adoptive families, it begins to grow into what the church was always meant to be.

How Do We Live It Together?

Robert and Shelley Bedford adopted Xander, who had both Down syndrome and autism. The Bedfords' friends at church learned that when Xander entered a new environment or felt insecure, he loved the comfort of rocking himself.

So, from the very first time the Bedfords attended church with their new son, the ushers made sure a rocking chair was waiting in the sanctuary for Xander. If the ushers forgot, someone else always seemed to notice and the chair quickly appeared.

This meant the Bedfords could sit together in church without having to leave when Xander was inevitably "done" being there. Week after week, Xander rocked through the service.

Xander needed that rocking chair for an entire year. Today, he attends with his family without needing the chair.

That rocking chair helped a precious boy feel at peace. It helped his family know they were not alone but loved and supported. And I suspect it helped many others in the church, too, to *see* deep truths about Christian community and God Himself. It made grace touchable.

Not every Christian is called to adopt . . . to foster . . . to mentor a child. But every Christian community *is* called to live out the pure religion described by James that includes caring for orphans and widows. The church *together* becomes home for the child in need of one. And each member of the body can play a part.

It's young adults babysitting. Empty nesters helping with errands. Fellow moms stopping by with a meal. Often, support for families rises organically—especially when encouraged from the pulpit and facilitated by a thoughtful coordinator who matches needs with willing helpers.

A lawyer in Seattle offers low- and no-cost legal help to families in his church and the surrounding area that are adopting or fostering.[23] An orthodontist in Colorado does the same with braces. Many churches have adoption support funds through groups such as Lifesong for Orphans and the ABBA Fund.

This kind of tangible help is invaluable. And more significant, it unequivocally affirms, *"You are wanted here."* Especially for families embracing children with special needs or other challenges, this feeling is often in short supply.

Such affirmation is especially meaningful in the hard times. I'll never forget how our church wrapped around my family when the girl we were adopting, precious Ayana Rachel, died suddenly of pneumonia. Although Ayana would never leave her home country of Ethiopia, our church held a funeral to celebrate her life and mourn together.

This grace is visible in the Sunday school teacher who patiently bears with the child who hasn't learned yet to sit still in a group setting. It's seen in the person down the pew who doesn't cast glances at the fidgeting child, but rather whispers to his foster mom, "It's okay—we're glad he's here!" It's the couple that invites the family with a wheelchair for a BBQ, even if it feels awkward at first.

These "little" things make a world of difference. Not only the practical help, important as that is; it's the feeling that others are in it with you. Taken together, it preaches without words: "God embraces us in the 'special needs' we *all* have—so we seek to do the same!"

What Grows a Culture?

What grows a culture of adoption and orphan care? Many things are useful. But underneath it all, three ingredients are essential:

First, a vision rooted in the gospel. We all need help to *see* the deep need and opportunity around us—and to *feel* how much God loves each vulnerable child, beginning with ourselves. We need to *hear* His clear call to care for these children, not merely as a "cause," but as a natural outgrowth of discipleship to Christ. Most of all, we need to grasp how loving orphans mirrors the way God first loved us. It makes the gospel visible! This vision can initially take root in laypersons. But to become the culture of a church, teaching from the pulpit is invaluable.

Second, practical support for families. Only a fraction of church members will actually foster, adopt, or mentor children. But each person can play a role. This starts with an attitude of hospitality, especially for children with unique challenges. Active support for families rises organically from this attitude, especially when it is modeled by church leadership. But providing organization to the support also helps. This can be as simple as designating a person who will identify and match willing helpers with specific needs. Some churches go much further—offering foster/adoption training, parental support groups, a regular "parents night out," and more. Within such tangible support, the culture grows from individual families to the entire church community. We become home for these children *together.*

Third, a theology of perseverance. Love for orphans is indeed redemptive. It can transform the lives of all involved. But alongside matchless gifts, it also involves *suffering with.* When we welcome into our hearts and intimate spaces young lives that have known great hurt, we taste of that hurt, too. Healing will often be slow, and sometimes less than we'd hoped. Like God's adoption of us, loving wounded children involves great cost. A healthy culture of adoption and orphan care speaks regularly and frankly about this, both in preparation for the journey and amidst it. When the culture of a church has embraced this truth, we can both struggle and celebrate with transparency. We bear together both the joy and the ache of it all.

What Happens in the Church?

As a church wraps around adoptive and foster families, something changes. Perhaps more than ever before, we feel a real *need* for each other. Communal life goes deeper. What was once polite conversation and typical social exchange becomes myriad threads of mutual service and prayer.

Arturo Barrientos is a pastor in Costa Rica. He marvels at how his church's community life has grown over the past several years as a culture of adoption and foster care took root. "Of course, there is a specific family in the church directly responsible for the child," he describes. "But the whole church becomes a family that also prays, and cares and loves and even helps financially for the good of the child."

Arturo's church had always ministered to the community. But this was like nothing else they'd ever experienced. "These children cease[d] being numbers in a document or photographs in a magazine or someone's project. Instead, in the midst of the church they are a living reality that touches and challenges hearts in a personal way."

The impact, he explains, spills outward from there. One of the children fostered in the church was eventually adopted by a family from outside the church. In saying goodbye to the girl, the whole church wept. "I have never seen so many tears," said Arturo. (With a twinkle in his eye, he added, "Not even for my best sermon.")

Months later, Arturo encountered the girl's adoptive parents in a mall. Their lives, too, had been changed. "I believe in God again," explained the father, "because there are churches and people like you that love and care for people like her."

On Christmas Day, that family of three attended Arturo's church. They stood in front of the congregation to thank every member of the church for playing a part in loving the little girl who was now their daughter. At the end of the service, Arturo's heart sang as he watched the congregation join in prayer for the family, arms outstretched in blessing.

This, Arturo concluded, is what the church is meant to be.

Watching Out for Pitfalls

Anyone who dares to wade near any deep human need will be—whether sooner or later—punctured by disappointment. That's true in efforts to engage human trafficking, disease or poverty . . . and in serving orphans, too. We've had such high hopes of *fixing* things. But the dilemmas are far more complex than we dreamed. Results are rarely all we hoped. Our best efforts may even have caused harm.

Gripping this truth starts us at a healthy place. Not paralyzed by fear. But at least a little suspicious of things we assume . . . trendy solutions . . . and even our own motives. We'll still inevitably make mistakes along the way. But with a humble, learning heart, we can avoid many of the big pitfalls. Here are several important ways to do that:

Speak of both the beauty and the brokenness. It's easy for advocates for any good thing to become cheerleaders—glossing over the hard things and implying, "just a little love will fix any hurt." A healthy culture of adoption and orphan care consistently speaks of *both* joy and heartache, much like the Psalms. It tells hard stories alongside the lovely ones, celebrates lives transformed and mourns at how tenacious brokenness can be.[24]

Take risks of corruption seriously. Money is often necessary to solutions. It provides micro loans for poor entrepreneurs, subsidizes foster care, and covers legitimate costs of adoption. But money also bends things toward itself. So any time money enters the picture, immense caution is needed. We must anticipate and guard against the ways money can incentivize poor judgment and bad action. Every effort to address need—from inter-country adoption and local foster care to global partnerships—must have strong accountability built in to its finances or corruption will likely result.

Be attentive to the voice of adult adoptees. Adoption typically centers on children at first. But, of course, our desire is always that girls and boys will grow into thriving adults. A healthy culture of adoption listens carefully to these voices as they grow. It speaks *with*, not just *about*, adoptees. Each adopted person's journey is different. Some see adoption as having defined their lives; others see it as just one thread in a larger tapestry. Some view adoption as rich in blessing; others trace their deepest wounds back to adoption; for still others, it is all of the above. But for any adoptee, to find listening ears and a welcoming heart signals that—whatever their perspective—adult adoptees are a welcome, valued, and *needed* part of the church community.

Don't underestimate the role of material poverty. Too often, it is poverty that carries children to orphanages, not the absence of parents.[25] The promise of things parents cannot afford—whether education, food, or otherwise—can be enough to sever otherwise healthy families. The same can happen in inter-country adoption, too. So it's vital to press hard on the question, "Could financial help or other basic supports enable this child to thrive in his family of birth?" If the answer is yes, that always needs to be the first priority.

Don't overestimate the role of material poverty. A comprehensive review of research on care options for children found that children were much more likely to thrive when moved out of low-nurture orphanages and into adoptive or foster families. But then came a surprise: when children with living parents were moved from orphanages back into their biological families, they often fared nearly as badly as those remaining in institutions.[26] Why? A big reason is that financial poverty is often intertwined with far more complex issues, from addiction and abuse to exploitation. Reunifying severed families should be the goal whenever safely possible. But so doing without grasping the deeper issues involved can bring great harm to children.

Respect birth parents. When focused on children, it can be easy to ignore biological parents. In adoption, they're often overlooked. In foster care, they can be vilified for ways they've hurt their children. A healthy culture of adoption and orphan care chooses otherwise. It honors mothers who give life to their children, offering support whether they opt to parent or plan for adoption. In foster care, it prays for the healing of the *whole* family, and supports that however it can.[27]

A Countercultural Name Worth Earning

A culture of adoption and orphan care is not abstract theology, at least not for long. It paints vivid pictures of God's heart. It makes the gospel touchable.

This touchable gospel has always defined the church at its best. Around AD 200, the apologist Tertullian wrote, "It is our care for the helpless, our practice of loving kindness, that brands us in the eyes of many of our opponents."[28]

Beautiful. May all Christians be described with such words!

To be sure, even when faithfully reflecting the heart of Jesus, we will still face trials and disapproval. Our Lord was crucified, after all. And He promised His disciples much the same.

Yet what could be more potentially healing for those who've been turned from God by false Christianity than for vibrant Christians to reflect God's true heart by loving orphans and foster youth? Imagine the church defined especially by this: *an extraordinary hospitality for children the world has cast aside.*

The Church as Family

Remember the girl from foster care in Tennessee—Chey—whose car burned up because no one told her about checking oil?

A mechanic at a Baptist church that Chey sometimes attended heard what happened. He helped her find a replacement, with the church making up the costs Chey could not afford. The mechanic also taught Chey all about car maintenance.

Later, when it looked like Chey would be forced to live in a group home, several people in the church worked on a plan to find her a family. A widow named Sherry, who'd taught Chey in seventh grade Sunday school, invited Chey to live with her.

It wasn't always easy. Chey was used to no rules. She pushed hard against limits Sherry set. But those boundaries came with love. "There was a lot of friction," Chey explains. "But if you ask me who my mom is today, I will tell you it's Sherry Hunter."

Others in the church kept loving Chey, too—including a lawyer, a nurse, and a teacher. Each helped with the unique gifts they had. "They worked behind the scenes to make sure I was getting what I needed," described Chey. "And when there was an issue they were always on call."

A few years ago, Chey met a great guy named Zach. When they decided to get married, that Baptist church was the obvious place. Chey came down the aisle in white, beaming. There was no father there to give her away. So the church had planned something else. When the pastor asked, "Who gives this woman to be married to this man?" the congregation rose and declared proudly together, "We do!"

"They were and are my family," explains Chey. "The most important part is that they showed me God's love. It's because of them that I understand how much He must love me."

Discussion Questions

. . . .

1. In what ways do you think orphan care and adoption will look different when they are rooted deeply in discipleship rather than just a "good cause"?

2. What do you see as the most important role(s) of the church in walking with families that adopt and foster?

3. Which of the three essential elements—vision, practical support, and theology of perseverance—is strongest at your church? Which needs the most work and what is one step you can take to help here?

4. What things would you especially want your church to be known for? How might a culture of adoption and orphan care contribute to that?

5. What are some potential pitfalls that churches need to be aware of as they engage in orphan care and adoption?

CHAPTER

5

What Does
the Culture Say?

Jim Daly and Kelly Rosati

I (JIM) HAVE OFTEN DESCRIBED MY CHILDHOOD AS A TRAIN wreck. It was not without its moments of happiness—but the memories that stand out most starkly are characterized by grief, fear, abandonment, insecurity, and loneliness. My parents divorced when I was five, my mom died of cancer when I was nine, and my stepdad cleared out our house and took off while my siblings and I were at our mother's funeral. My time in foster care was equally troubled, to put it mildly.

My heart for orphans and my intense compassion for children who need homes grew out of my own deep longing to be part of a stable, loving family. It would be impossible to overstate the desire every child feels to belong, to feel safe, and to know the unconditional love of a mother and a father. Those rank among the most basic emotional needs of children, and when they go unmet it can wreak havoc in a child's heart and soul.

While I'm fortunate that the Lord carried me through my own difficult early experiences and used them to shape me into the husband and father I am today, I also know that my story, unfortunately, isn't unique. Millions of children around the globe go to bed each night hungry, or battered, or alone—maybe all three.

According to a report issued by the United States Aid to International Development (USAID), there are 17.8 million children around the world who have lost *both* parents, and at least two million of those classified as "highly vulnerable children" have been placed in institutional care. The report adds that "unknown numbers [of children] are surviving without families." We've all seen the heartbreaking images of precious little ones in far-flung countries—solitary, malnourished children whose only meals will be whatever scraps they can salvage from the local community dump. And although not every orphan's circumstances are quite as desperate as that, any child living without a family suffers want and privation in one way or another.

It's difficult to wrap our minds around the sheer numbers of children trying to survive without the love and protection of parents. And yet we must not look away, not if we hope to help.

What Has Been the Solution?

So what *is* the solution to such heart-wrenching need? That depends on whom you ask.

Many Christians will respond by holding out adoption as a wonderful way to "visit orphans . . . in their affliction" (James 1:27 ESV). And while the last several years have brought about an encouraging resurgence of evangelical involvement in orphan care, the church's ministry toward orphaned children is nothing new. From time immemorial, God's people have cared for children without parents.

Dr. John Aloisi of Detroit Baptist Theological Seminary has penned a fascinating paper that details orphan care throughout church history. He describes not only the broader evangelical participation in orphan care from the early church on, but also the stories of famed figures such as Martin Luther, John Calvin, George Whitefield, and, of course, George Müller—all of whom personally took orphaned children under their wings.

Martin Luther and his wife adopted four children whose mother had died of the plague. What's more, they cared for seven orphaned nieces and nephews. When John Calvin's wife died, he continued to serve as a father to her children—his stepchildren—although society at the time likely would have deemed it acceptable for a widowed man to turn his stepchildren over to another couple or even to an institution. Nonetheless, he raised them as if they were his biological children, and he also served as guardian for several other youngsters who had lost their fathers.

Several generations later, Whitefield and Müller both established orphanages that would become safe havens for numerous fatherless children. Whitefield cared for dozens of orphaned children, and Müller provided for a staggering *ten thousand* children over the course of his lifetime.

Such acts of charity, as they might have been called, likely were not debated or critiqued at the time—they were simply considered part and parcel of the Christian calling to care for "the least of these." In fact, with the possible exception of Müller, the others mentioned here are not widely known for their care of orphaned children. Most twenty-first-century believers are probably unaware that so many well-known preachers and theologians were personally invested in orphan care. Could it be that it didn't make headlines back then because it was simply expected that the people of God would do all they could to ensure that orphans had homes? Consider these words of Polycarp, the second-century bishop of Smyrna,

> The presbyters, for their part, must be compassionate, merciful to all, turning back those who have gone astray, visiting all the sick, not neglecting a widow, orphan, or poor person, but always aiming at what is honorable in the sight of God and of people. (Polycarp, Philippians 6.1, c. AD 110)

Apparently, the early Christians considered orphan care, among other good works, to be synonymous with serving God and His people honorably. That view may still be prevalent with many believers, but it could be argued that we've lost the urgency that once roused the body of Christ to ensure that orphans were receiving the church's care and protection. That's why it's so heartening to see an increasing awareness throughout Christendom of the global plight of orphans and a renewed commitment to the church's mandate to stand in the gap for these defenseless children.

What Does the Solution Appear to Be?

Today's culture at large, however, often accuses Christians of having less than savory motives when it comes to adoption. Somehow, those who want to open their hearts and homes to needy children are either part of some elaborate "proselytizing" scheme or want their kids to serve as poster children for the adoption alternative to abortion. (That evangelism and pro-life ministry are seen as problematic is simply one more indication of the cultural drift away from biblical morality.)

Be that as it may, neither charge is logical. Think of the adoptive families you may know. Given all of the time, expense, and scrutiny they endured throughout the adoption process—not to mention the significant adjustment afterward—it's hard to imagine that anything other than the deepest and most profound love for their adopted children played a role in their decision to adopt.

Child evangelism can be achieved in numerous ways, and the pro-life movement is being carried out courageously on many fronts. Adoption, however, is an entirely distinct calling that requires a lifetime of sacrifice and commitment. And we would venture to say that those who heed this call do so for reasons far removed from the kinds of agendas and ulterior motives suggested by certain individuals and groups across the culture.

Of course, most Christians would readily acknowledge that sharing the gospel with their children—both biological and adopted—is at the top of their list of priorities. *Any* couple, regardless of their religious beliefs, wants to instill their own values and beliefs in their kids. That's a universal aspect of parenting. It's certainly not unique to Christian adoptive parents. Somehow, though, the culture would label it suspect.

One writer leading the charge to challenge the evangelical adoption movement is Kathryn Joyce, an author and journalist. In a 2013 op-ed that appeared in the *New York Times*, Joyce claims that a growing awareness of the needs of orphans and the church's eagerness to meet that need have led to greater abuses and corruptions related to international adoptions. According to Joyce,

> . . . some movement insiders say that evangeli-
> cals—whether driven by zeal or naïveté—have had

a disproportionate impact on the international
adoption system. . . . For too long, well-meaning
Americans have brought their advocacy and money
to bear on an adoption industry that revolves around
Western demand.[29]

Joyce argues that, given the financial incentive involved, many foreign governments resort to deceptive and even criminal methods to match children with interested couples. No one's denying the existence of unscrupulous and exploitive practices on the part of those who stand to gain monetarily by adoption. That has always been the case, and probably always will be. But to paint adoption with such a broad brush is to disregard those organizations that are working diligently to promote adoption *and* take steps to safeguard children from the kinds of wrongdoing that have garnered so much attention in the media. It also overlooks the immeasurable benefit of adoption to children genuinely in need of permanent homes.

Indeed, what Joyce seems to ignore are the thousands of previously orphaned children who were tucked into bed by loving moms and dads last night—children who know there will be a meal for them when they wake, hugs from parents before they head off to school, and a future of hopeful tomorrows with families who love them. When this happens for just one child it should be celebrated—that it's taking place all over the world because caring Christians want to help meet a genuine need is cause for wholehearted rejoicing.

Christians who are interested in orphan care are often charged, as well, with neglecting to address poverty and family breakdown—two epidemics that lend themselves significantly to the orphan crisis. Evangelical organizations, however, are on the front lines of both poverty relief and family preservation, here at home and around the world. Our own international outreach through Focus on the Family is geared toward strengthening families across the globe.

But that kind of work is being done with the realization that, even with the most effective humanitarian efforts to keep families intact and lift needy people out of poverty, there will always be children who need homes.

Happily Ever After?

Aside from the broader society's assessments about the merits of adoption, it's interesting to look elsewhere in the culture to discover commonly held views on the subject. It's hard to find a more telling indicator of popular opinion than offerings coming out of Hollywood, which has made adoption the subject of numerous films.

Think of *Annie*, the beloved musical-turned-film in which a precocious young orphan captures the heart of a surly millionaire. Or *Anne of Green Gables*, which features the antics of a delightful and imaginative orphan who manages to win over her stern-faced guardian, Marilla. Or even *Despicable Me*, the animated tale of a notorious villain whose hard heart is eventually softened by three young orphan girls. These and numerous other films provide touching portrayals of the joy of adoption and its life-changing impact on both the children and adoptive parents involved.

While it's wonderful that so many heart-warming movies about adoption are being produced, notice what is often a common thread in some of the most popular adoption-related films. A charming, affectionate, winsome child—who seems almost unfazed by experiences of neglect, abandonment, and abuse—waits eagerly for a family. Meanwhile, a gruff and churlish adult with no interest whatsoever in children becomes unexpectedly attached to an orphan and is soon transformed into a loving and devoted parent. This scenario obviously doesn't describe all movies about adoption, but it's certainly a well-loved plot line.

There's no doubt that adoptive parents are touched and changed by the experience of adoption. However, a self-centered and ill-tempered adult is unlikely to change overnight into a parent with the wisdom, love, and patience needed to care for a wounded child. And we can be equally certain that children who have suffered the kinds of deprivation and loneliness experienced by so many orphans will have the scars to show for it.

It's also worth noting that, when it comes to films dealing with adoption, more often than not it's the events leading up to the adoption that comprise the plot. Adoption, then, becomes the happy ending.

In reality, though, signing those adoption papers is simply the beginning. It's the start of many joys, but many challenges as well—particularly for those who adopt an older child or a child with special needs. Is it worth it? Absolutely. Is it easy? Definitely not. And we do a disservice to prospective adoptive parents when we claim that it is.

Our Adoption Stories

I (Kelly) am passionate about portraying for people the beauty and joy of adoption while also educating them about its challenges. Many wonder how those two realities can work in tandem, but my own family is proof positive that it's more than possible. My husband and I adopted our four children from the foster care system, and we can attest to the struggles of parenting kids who come to us with emotional scars that most of us can't begin to fathom.

Those of us who have adopted children bruised—either literally or figuratively—by their past experiences have our work cut out for us, to be sure. We will endure feelings of isolation, confusion, and indecision. We will wrestle to strike a balance between showering our children with love and drawing much-needed lines at unacceptable or dangerous behavior. For children from other countries, we will strive to help our children with cultural assimilation in their new homeland while continuing to honor the traditions of their birth country.

We will, in short, take on a herculean task. And nothing less than the extravagant grace and abundant strength of God will be required if we are to run well this unique race. Raising kids who bear deep wounds takes endless love, patience, and trust in a God who creates beauty out of ashes. And despite the hard days and unique challenges, it is wholly and undeniably worth it.

Unfortunately, however, we live at a time when society struggles to marry hardship with joy. If something requires sacrifice, too many will dismiss it as not worth the trouble—when, in truth, struggle and perseverance often form the very pathway to lasting joy and fulfillment.

What's more, if we look at the very heart of adoption, we can see a relationship that mirrors the believer's adoption as a son or daughter of God. There's nothing to compare with the biblical theology of sonship—which paints a picture of orphans who have been adopted into a forever family, redeemed from slavery, rescued from darkness, and brought into the light of God's grace. What a breathtaking narrative of salvation.

Isn't it interesting that, in the well-known mandate found in James 1:27, we are pointed to two demographic groups—widows and orphans—and instructed to care particularly for them? Aside from the very real needs of widows and orphans (especially at the time the epistle was penned), it seems that our ministry to those who can give nothing back is uniquely important to God. Perhaps because that type of self-sacrificing outreach—including adoption—reflects the very heart of God when He sent His only Son to take on flesh and submit to a torturous death so that He could gather His undeserving children to Himself.

In short, there are few earthly relationships that represent the gospel more movingly than adoption. It is a beautiful picture of belonging and hope. As Brian Ivie, director of the Focus on the Family film *The Drop Box*, put it, "I'm hoping people see a type of love that spends itself on behalf of others and doesn't expect anything back. Because that's what God's love is like."[30]

The love of an adoptive parent is powerful enough to cross oceans to claim a hurting and lonely child. It's steadfast enough to endure sleepless nights, psychiatrist sessions, and academic struggles. And it is rooted in a hope that looks beyond any immediate adversity toward the day when healing will begin to take shape in a wounded child's heart and soul.

Pastor Jong-rak Lee, whose incredible outreach is portrayed in *The Drop Box*, epitomizes that kind of compassion and "all in" love. When he learned how many infants were being abandoned in the streets of Seoul, South Korea, he was moved to help. He developed a "drop box" and invited women to place their babies there rather than leaving them in the streets where they would almost surely die. He and his wife have since adopted many of those infants.

On the face of it, Pastor Lee's circumstances might seem unsustainable. He and his wife live humbly, deal with almost constant exhaustion and chronic health issues, and rely on the Lord's tangible support from day to day. Moreover, there's no end in sight—because their devotion to the singular mission they've been given is unflagging.

However, despite the hardship that accompanies the vital work they're doing, the Lees radiate a joy and contentment that can only come from the assurance that they are carrying out a divine mandate. And each and every one of their children is a source of boundless love and deep fulfillment for them.

When *The Drop Box* hit screens across North America, Pastor Lee's story resonated deeply with viewers. Many contacted us to say that the film had changed their lives and to ask how they could engage with the issue of orphan care. When Pastor Lee humbly prayed that the Lord would give him these babies— babies who were too often viewed as nameless and disposable— little did he know that his story would be used around the world to galvanize so many of his fellow believers to action.

We've heard from those who have been prompted to support the Lees' ministry, to partner with adoption care ministries, or even to initiate the adoption process personally. Pastor Lee is a powerful example of the immeasurable difference one person can make in the world.

Changing the Culture, One Adoption at a Time

Numerous other individuals and Christian organizations are also working diligently and tirelessly to come alongside orphaned children. If you ask any of the people connected with these efforts what drives them, it's unlikely they would respond by saying they are energized by their loyalty to a particular "cause." Instead, they are moved by the children themselves, each one created for a purpose and given inherent and inestimable worth.

For our part, at Focus on the Family we are doing all we can to help pair needy children with willing parents. Toward that end, our team developed its Wait No More initiative as a means of informing, equipping, and mobilizing churches to come alongside children in the foster care system. With three hundred thousand American churches to a hundred thousand kids in US foster care awaiting adoption, finding homes for these kids is an altogether attainable goal.

As Christian recording artist and adoption advocate Steven Curtis Chapman put it,

> If only seven percent of the two billion Christians in
> the world would care for a single orphan in dis-
> tress, there would effectively be no more orphans. If

everybody would be willing to simply do something to care for one of these precious treasures, I think we would be amazed by just how much we could change the world.[31]

At the time of this writing, more than three thousand families have initiated adoption from foster care after attending one of Focus on the Family's Wait No More events. That is an extremely promising start, but we remain keenly aware that there is more work to be done to alleviate the suffering of orphans, both stateside and around the world.

Conclusion

As we strive to serve as the hands and feet of Christ to orphaned children, it's also our hope that God will enable us to play a role in correcting some of the cultural misperceptions that exist with regard to adoption. All too often, adopted children are seen as second-class members of their families. These kids might be asked where their "real" parents are, and adoptive parents might face questions about when they're going to have a "child of their own." In most cases, these types of inquiries are probably well-meaning, but that doesn't make them any less hurtful—because at their heart they betray a thinking that devalues the true nature of adoption. And they shed light on a culture that often can't make sense of those who give without expecting anything in return.

Adoption is nothing less than a love that pours itself out for another in a million ways, both big and small, without regard for any earthly reward or acclaim. While that kind of sacrifice may be a mystery to those who have not yet experienced the lavish grace of God, it remains one of the church's highest of callings.

Discussion Questions

1. When you learn that a couple you know has chosen to adopt, what kinds of assumptions do you find yourself making about their reasons for making that decision?

2. What are some of the challenges adoptive parents may face after bringing home their children? How might those challenges be intensified in the case of children with special needs or traumatic backgrounds?

3. What are some ways that believers can offer practical support and encouragement to the adoptive families in their midst?

4. How does adoption present us with a clear picture of the gospel?

5. Why do you suppose some people see adoption as God's "Plan B"? How can the church play a role in casting a vision for adoption as the Lord's best and first plan for many families?

ADDITIONAL READING

Adopted for Life by Russell Moore

Becoming Home: Adoption, Foster Care, and Mentoring—Living Out God's Heart for Orphans by Jedd Medefind

Orphanology: Awakening to Gospel-Centered Adoption and Orphan Care by Tony Merida and Rick Morton

Wait No More: One Family's Amazing Adoption Journey by Kelly Rosati and John Rosati

Finding Home: An Imperfect Path to Faith and Family by Jim Daly

ACKNOWLEDGMENTS

TO THE MANY HANDS INSIDE AND OUTSIDE THE ERLC, WE thank you for your help and assistance on this book. The ERLC team provided joyful encouragement in the planning and execution of this series, and without them, it would never have gotten off the ground. We want to also personally thank Phillip Bethancourt who was a major visionary behind this project. We'd also like to thank Jennifer Lyell and Devin Maddox at B&H, our publisher, for their work in guiding us through this process.

ABOUT THE ERLC

THE ERLC IS DEDICATED TO ENGAGING THE CULTURE WITH the gospel of Jesus Christ and speaking to issues in the public square for the protection of religious liberty and human flourishing. Our vision can be summed up in three words: kingdom, culture, and mission.

Since its inception, the ERLC has been defined around a holistic vision of the kingdom of God, leading the culture to change within the church itself and then as the church addresses the world. The ERLC has offices in Washington, DC, and Nashville, Tennessee.

ABOUT THE CONTRIBUTORS

Jim Daly is president of Focus on the Family and host of the *Daily Broadcast*, heard by more than 2.9 million listeners a week on more than a thousand radio stations across the U.S.

Jedd Medefind serves as president of the Christian Alliance for Orphans (www.cafo.org), a community of ministries and churches that work together to inspire and equip Christians for orphan care, foster care, and adoption. Previously, Jedd led the White House Office of Faith-Based and Community Initiatives for President George W. Bush. His most recent book is *Becoming Home: Adoption, Foster Care and Mentoring—Living Out God's Heart for the Orphan.*

Russell Moore is president of the Ethics and Religious Liberty Commission of the Southern Baptist Convention, the nation's largest Protestant denomination. He is the author of several books, including the *Christianity Today* 2016 Book of the Year, *Onward: Engaging Culture without Losing the Gospel*. He and his wife Maria are the parents of five sons.

David Prince is the pastor of preaching and vision at Ashland Avenue Baptist Church in Lexington, Kentucky. He also serves as assistant professor of Christian Preaching at The Southern Baptist Theological Seminary in Louisville, Kentucky.

Kelly Rosati is the vice president of Community Outreach at Focus on the Family where she serves as the ministry spokesperson on child advocacy issues. Rosati oversees the Adoption and Orphan Care Initiative, the Sanctity of Human Life department, Option Ultrasound, and Community Care efforts.

Randy Stinson is the senior vice president for Academic Administration and Provost; professor of Leadership and Family Ministry at The Southern Baptist Theological Seminary in Louisville, Kentucky. He and his wife, Danna, have been married since 1991 and have eight children: Gunnar, Georgia, Fisher, Eden, Payton, Spencer, Willa, and Brewer.

NOTES

1. J. I. Packer, *Knowing God* (Downers Grove, IL: InterVarsity Press, 1973), 209.

2. Ibid., 206–207.

3. For an additional work that expands on the issues discussed in this chapter, see Russell D. Moore, *Adopted for Life: The Priority of Adoption for Christian Families and Churches*, 2nd ed. (Wheaton, IL: Crossway, 2015).

4. This quote came from a source document of *Didascalia Apostolorum,* known as *Testamentum Domini Nostri Jesu Christi.* (Ed. Arthur Voobus, *The Synodicon in the West Syrian Tradition*, CSCO 367 and 368, Scriptores Syri 161 and 162 [Louvain: Secretariat du CorpusSCO, 1975], 12 [Syriac] and 35 [English]).

5. Seneca, in "To Novatus on Anger," Book I, chapter 15.

6. Code of Justinian, 8.52.2.

7. According to the annual "State of Giving Report" by the Evangelical Council for Financial Accountability, year over year growth in giving by Christians in the category of "Orphan Care" has risen near or above 12 percent each year. According to the annual data released by the Center for Philanthropy at Indiana University, overall charitable giving by Americans rose between 3 and 4 percent during each of those years.

8. There are roughly 100,000 children waiting for adoptive families in America and it is estimated there are 330,000+ churches. The total number of children in foster care is roughly 415,000. So it

can also be said that, "If each US church adopted just one child and fostered just one child, there'd be no children waiting for adoptive or foster families in America."

9. Details and quotes drawn from Bishop Martin's book, *Small Town, Big Miracle*; the article "Miracle in Possum Trot" in *Charisma Magazine,* May 1, 2010; and Bishop W. C. Martin's live interview at the Christian Alliance for Orphans' Summit IX on May 2, 2013.

10. Statistics related to orphans are often misquoted and misunderstood. To learn more about the numbers (and what they do and do not accurately reveal), see the CAFO publication, "On Understanding Orphan Statistics," available as a free PDF online: https://cafo.org /wp-content/uploads/2015/06/Christian-Alliance-for-Orphans-_On -Understanding-Orphan-Statistics_.pdf.

11. It is essential to connect the biblical concept of the "orphan"/ "fatherless" to all of these situations, helping Christians grasp that *these* are children God calls us to care for and defend. However, when speaking of specific situations, it is also important to use terms that are most accurate and avoid giving offense. For example, it is generally unhelpful (and can even be hurtful) to use the term "orphan" when speaking of a child in US foster care.

12. Mark E. Courtney, et al., "Midwest Evaluation of the Adult Functioning of Former Foster Youth: Outcomes at Age 26" (University of Chicago: Chapin Hall, 2011), http://www.chapinhall.org/research /report/midwest-evaluation-adult-functioning-former-foster-youth.

13. Erik Eckholm, "Study Finds More Woes Following Foster Care," *New York Times*, April 7, 2010.

14. "Rebuilding a life: A young girl struggles to overcome the trauma of trafficking," UNICEF, May 25, 2012, http://www.unicef .org/infobycountry/moldova_24121.html.

15. A. C. S. Mushingeh, et al., "HIV/AIDS and Child Labour in Zambia: A rapid assessment on the case of the Lusaka, Copperbelt and Eastern Provinces," Paper No. 5, (Geneva/Lusaka: International

Labour Organization, International Programme on the Elimination of Child Labour, August 2002).

16. Malika Saada Saar, "Stopping the Foster Care to Child Trafficking Pipeline," *The Huffington Post*, updated *January 23, 2014.*

17. For example, a meta-study covering nineteen countries found an IQ difference of more than 20 points between children in orphanages and those in families (van IJzendoorn, et al., "IQ of Children Growing Up in Children's Homes").

18. Quote from Christina Groark and Robert McCall's "Implementing changes in institutions to improve young children's development" (St. Petersburg—USA orphanage research team, 2005).

19. See Jedd Medefind, *Becoming Home: Adoption, Foster Care, and Mentoring—Living Out God's Heart for Orphans* (Grand Rapids, MI: Zondervan, 2014), 24. Five percent of practicing Christians have adopted versus 2 percent for the general population. As-yet unpublished data from this same Barna polling discovered that this number is even higher—10 percent—when for evangelical Christians.

20. Ibid. Three percent of practicing Christians have fostered versus 2 percent overall. Roughly the same ratio is seen when asked if they "probably" or "definitely" will foster in the next five years: 15 percent versus 11 percent. (This latter statistic comes from the same Barna polling highlighted in *Becoming Home* but has not yet been published.)

21. Ibid.

22. Casey Foster Family Assessment Training Workbook, quoted by Jayne Schooler in "Why Are Foster Parents Leaving?" *Fostering Families Today*, September/October 2009, 23.

23. This lawyer, Andrew Schneidler, aims to see Christians lawyers offer this kind of support in every state. Visit www.thepermanence project.org to learn more.

24. Speaking only of the beauty/joy of adoption can be an error. But it is possible to fall off the other side of the horse, too—dwelling only on the hard things and negative stories. As one reader of this manuscript (who has adopted several older children from orphanages)

reminded, "It will also be MORE than we ever imagined! Adopted children bring a new dimension to the family, teach biological children about the meaning of unconditional love, enhance and expand the worldview of a family, add new talents, perspectives, and joys! Our family would be SO much less rich in love and texture and joy without our 'adopted' children. It has enhanced us all and shown us beauty we didn't even know we were missing!"

25. While varying greatly by region, it is estimated that from 20 percent to as high as 90 percent of children in orphanages have a surviving parent or relative. Certainly, many of these parents and relatives are unable or unwilling to care for these children. But for at least a portion, material poverty was a primary factor leading to the child's placement in an orphanage.

26. M. M. Julian and R. B. McCall, "The development of children within different alternative residential care environments," *International Journal of Child and Family Welfare* 14 (2011): 119–47.

27. An excellent model for supporting biological families is the Safe Families program. Learn more at www.safe-families.org.

28. This version of the quote is drawn originally from James Moffatt's translation of Adolf Von Harnack, *The Expansion of Christianity in the First Three Centuries*, Volume 1 (New York, NY: G. P. Putnam's Sons, 1904), 184. Other translations have slight variations on the original quote from Tertullian's Apology, section XXXIX.

29. Kathyrn Joyce, "The Evangelical Orphan Boom," *New York Times*, September 21, 2013, http://www.nytimes.com/2013/09/22/opinion/sunday/the-evangelical-orphan-boom.html?_r=0.

30. See http://dropbox.focusonthefamily.ca/behind-the-story.

31. Steven Curtis Chapman, "Commentary: Our Tragedy and God's Love for Orphans," CNN, August 8, 2008, http://www.cnn.com/2008/SHOWBIZ/Music/08/07/chapman.orphans/index.html?iref=mpstoryview.